PUTTING ON BLUE

Confederates from the Athens, Georgia, Area
Who Became Galvanized Yankees

Al Hester, PhD

To: CAROL LEE

THANKS SO MUCH
FOR ALL YOUR HELP!

Al Hester
12-13-15

ATHENS HISTORICAL SOCIETY

A Co-Sponsored Publication
by the Athens Historical Society & The Green Berry Press

To the brave men, North and South,
who fought the Civil War

Copyright © 2015 by Albert Lee Hester
Published by The Green Berry Press,
184 Milledge Terrace
Athens, Georgia, 30606 U.S.A
All rights reserved,
Except those held by The Athens Historical Society
ISBN: 978-0-9966399-0-3
Printed and bound by Lightning Source, Inc.
On acid-free paper, meeting all ANSI standards
for archival quality (paper)
alhester@earthlink.net
706-543-9138

FRONT COVER: *Mounted Infantryman*, Frederic Remington. A mounted infantryman on duty in the West. Galvanized Yankees, as Union Army members, often served as mounted infantrymen fighting Indians. COURTESY OF ENCORE EDITIONS.

BACK COVER: *Attack on the Supply Train*, Frederic Remington. Union soldiers fight off an attack on a supply train. Galvanized Yankees frequently guarded wagon trains in the West. COURTESY OF WILD-WEST-ART.ORG UNDER CREATIVE COMMONS LICENSE. Map: Portion of the Clarke County area, 1846. COURTESY OF GEORGIAINFO.GALILEO.USG.EDU/TOPICS/COUNTIES/CLARKE.

Contents

List of Photographs, Engravings, and Illustrations (Gallery follows page 23.)

Preface

James K. Reap
The Athens Historical Society

AS COMMEMORATION of the sesquicentennial of the Civil War draws to a close, the Athens Historical Society is pleased to partner with Green Berry Press to bring you this monograph on Northeast Georgia's "Galvanized Yankees." These were captured Confederate soldiers who chose service in the Union Army, largely in the West, in exchange for release from deadly Northern prisons. This relatively little-known episode from the latter years of the War offers a distinctive insight into one of the epic and transformational events in American history and its impact on residents of Northeast Georgia.

The author, Al Hester, is noted in the Athens area for his research and writing on a variety of historical topics. In addition to sharing new insights on familiar subjects, he has brought often-neglected aspects of local history to light. In particular, he has contributed insightful articles to the Society's journal, the *Athens Historian,* and shared astute observations on local history at our public programs.

A key component of the Society's mission is the publication of historical materials that "promote and stimulate public interest in and appreciation of the history of Athens and related areas, and to develop in every way an understanding of their historical past." We believe this monograph furthers that goal in an engaging and accessible way and hope it assists the reader to gain a more complete view of the region's complex and fascinating history.

Introduction

Al Hester
Author and director of The Green Berry Press

IT IS A PLEASURE TO JOIN with the Athens Historical Society to bring this book to you. Knowledge of local history of our area is important to understand our past and the roots of the present day and future. As you read *Putting on Blue: Confederates from the Athens, Georgia, Area Who Became Galvanized Yankees,* you will become familiar with one of the most unusual developments of the Civil War and how it influenced some soldiers from Clarke County and adjacent counties.

The book is the story of 52 Confederate soldiers who were captured and placed in horrific Northern prisons with little hope for quick release to return home. The Lincoln administration offered them their freedom from prison if they would swear their allegiance to the Union and enlist in special regiments to serve in the West. This freed Union Regular Army troops to join the battle against the South in major areas of the war. The newly enlisted Southerners were called "Galvanized Yankees." They battled against Indian depredations, protected settlers and guarded trails and telegraph service during the last two years of the war and until November, 1866.

It is a story of mainly privates, the lowest rank of the military, from Clarke, Greene, Jackson, Madison, Morgan, Oglethorpe and Walton Counties. During the Civil War, these counties bordered on Clarke County. Oconee County had not yet been formed from Clarke County. These men were mainly farmers of small holdings and not usually members of the elite plantation families.

They weighed and measured carefully before deciding to forsake the Confederate service. They knew that to many of their comrades and fellow citizens they would be considered highly disloyal to the South. But thousands of Southern soldiers from the Southern states did choose freedom from perilous prisons to serve the Union. Many were eventually rewarded with Union military pensions.

While these men had at least a coating of loyalty to the Union, inside they were still Confederates, just as galvanized metals had a coating of protective metal on the outside to protect the steel beneath. Nevertheless, they for a time served generally as steadfast Union soldiers.

This book is a first co-sponsorship between the Athens Historical Society and the Green Berry Press. It is our hope to tell of these local Galvanized Yankees in a manner to encourage interest in local history and to give AHS members and the public enjoyment in a longer publication than the usual shorter historic articles in *The Athens Historian* periodical, published by the Society.

If readers like this book, it's our hope that other book-length or monograph-length historical topics will be forthcoming.

The Green Berry Press in 2001, joined by the Athens-Clarke Heritage Foundation, co-sponsored an Athens-Clarke Bicentennial Publication, *Athens Memories: The WPA Federal Writers' Project Interviews*, a collection of interviews of Athens area residents about their lives in the 1930s and earlier. I hope that the new book about the area's Galvanized Yankees will be as well received by local history lovers.

March, 2015
Athens, Georgia

PUTTING ON BLUE

*Confederates from the Athens, Georgia, Area
Who Became Galvanized Yankees*

Chapter 1

Who Were the Galvanized Yankees?

IN THE UNION'S CIVIL WAR military prison at Rock Island Barracks, Illinois, Confederate Pvt. John M. Whitmire, born in Jackson County, near Athens, was thinking hard. He was trying to figure out whether to stay a prisoner or to join the Yankee Army, serving in the West. The date was Oct. 15, 1864.[1]

In the Union prison at Bermuda Hundred, Virginia, Pvt. George W. Bone, another Confederate, giving his birthplace as Athens, pondered signing the Union loyalty oath to leave prison for U.S. service fighting Indians and protecting settlers in the West.[2]

Later, in the Yankee prison at Point Lookout, Maryland, one of George's brothers, Pvt. Matthew Bone, another Confederate soldier listing Athens as his birthplace, was also making up his mind to swear the oath of allegiance to the Union to get out of prison.[3]

All three of these from the Athens area decided to try their luck putting on the blue Yankee uniform—a tough choice. By changing sides in the war, they knew some at home would see them as traitors. But they might increase their chances of survival by leaving wretched Northern prisons.[4] They would join thousands of ex-Confederates, to become known as "Galvanized Yankees."

The Galvanized Yankees made up a little-known but significant group of Southern prisoners who volunteered to fight for the North to get out of prison. At least 7,000 to 8,000 ex-Confederates took the loyalty oath to the Union after they were captured and imprisoned.

1

Most of them were sent West to fight Indians, guard stagecoaches, settlers and telegraph lines, replacing Union soldiers during the last two years of the Civil War.[5]

I have located 52 Galvanized Yankees from Clarke County and its adjacent counties who decided to gamble on survival in blue uniforms. Galvanized Yankees played a major role on the Western frontier, taking the places of thousands of Union troops who couldn't be spared for frontier duties during the Civil War.

This book tells the story of this group of Georgians who became Galvanized Yankees—Yankees on the outside but Confederates on the inside. The term Galvanized Yankees became the usual name for these former enemies of the North who swore to serve in its military forces.[6] Galvanization was a common process at that time of coating steel with zinc to prevent rusting.

. . .

BOTH GEORGE AND MATTHEW lived in Athens as part of the James E. Bone family when the Civil War began. They and eight brothers volunteered to be Confederate soldiers. Theirs was a family with twenty-three children plus Mildred (Millie) Bone, their mother, and James E. Bone, their father.[7] Sixteen of the children—ten males and six females—were alive at the time of the Civil War. (See also Table 1, on page 44, showing the Bones' war service.)

The patriotic Bone family also furnished soldiers for the War of 1812 and the Mexican War, and it is a family tradition that Bone men fought in the American Revolution. James E. Bone received a pension for his War of 1812 service.[8] His son, Sanders Bone, obtained a pension for serving in the Mexican War.[9] Sanders also enlisted in the Confederate forces.

On April 7, 1863, Mildred Bone wrote a personal letter to Confederate Gen. Robert E. Lee, pleading for the discharge or furlough of at least one of her sons to help harvest the Bones' crops. The Bones were living near Boggs Chapel on the Jefferson River Road when she wrote to the general.[10] On April 18, 1863, General Lee replied:

"Mrs. Mildred Bone, Athens, Ga.—Dear Madame: Your letter of the 7th instant, asking the discharge or furlough for one of your sons, has been received. You have set a noble example in devoting your ten sons to the service of the country and in encouraging them to defend their homes. We need every good soldier we have in the army. If we allowed all to return who are needed at home we should soon have no country and no homes. I sympathize with you in your anxieties and privations, but I trust your kind neighbors in the patriotic state of Georgia will not permit you to want while your brave sons are doing their duty manfully against the enemy. I am, very respectfully, your obedient servant,

R. E. Lee, General

Mrs. Bone's efforts to get help from her sons in the Army and General Lee's response received coverage over the years in a number of U.S. newspapers. The *Athens* [Georgia] *Banner* printed the story and General Lee's letter on May 10, 1895. Dorcas Bone, an unmarried daughter of James and Mildred, had the original letter in her possession until her death on Aug. 22, 1911. Other papers across the nation also printed the story. The letter was lost after Dorcas Bone's death. An article containing Mrs. Bone's letter and General Lee's response was also published in the *New York Times* of May 15, 1895, which is available online.[11]

During the war, Mrs. Bone was on a Confederate government list in Athens indicating she had a family dependent upon a disabled Confederate soldier for family support, so perhaps Athens did affirm General Lee's faith that Mrs. Bone would receive aid from the community.[12]

Privates George and Matthew enlisted in Company "G" of the Twenty-Fifth North Carolina Infantry Regiment, as did their brother Jonathan. Quite a few Athens men joined this company, in the Twenty-Fifth, called the "Highland Regiment."[13] The well-liked Company "G" commander was Capt. William S. Grady, of Athens, father of the well known Henry Grady, who after the war was a spokesman for the "New South."

Private Whitmire, who had moved with his family to Alabama, enlisted in the Nineteenth Alabama Infantry Regiment. On Oct. 15, 1864, he joined the Third U.S. Volunteer Infantry Regiment to see Yankee duty in the West.[14] Whitmire's Union regiment was one of the First through Sixth U.S. Volunteer Infantry regiments, whose members were mainly Galvanized Yankees. These units were commanded by Regular Army officers, not by Galvanized Yankees.

George W. Bone decided to leave the Bermuda Hundred, Virginia, prison and to swear allegiance to the Union. The prison register notes "Oath Taken" by Bone.[15] The same document affirms that Bone was a "reb deserter." His desertion seems documented, but looking at his long service and wounding with his Confederate unit, he might have been separated from his company or was taken captive at the federal military headquarters at Bermuda Hundred. He enlisted in Company "E," Third Battalion of the Fifteenth U.S. Infantry Regiment, a few days after Private Whitmire's decision.[16]

No military records indicate in which U.S. unit Matthew Bone would serve, although his oath of loyalty to the Union and its army is on record. Matthew Bone chose loyalty to the Union on June 24, 1865, more than a month after Gen. Robert E. Lee's surrender at Appomattox, Virginia.[17] Scattered fighting continued for about ten weeks longer in the war.

The last Confederate general to surrender was Brig. Gen. Stand Watie of Georgia, leading Cherokee troops in Oklahoma, on June 23, 1865.[18] Nevertheless, one day later, we find Private Matthew Bone enlisted to serve in the Union Army. Confederate prisoners had no certainty concerning when they would be released. Many opted to join the Union Army even after Gen. Robert E. Lee's surrender on April 9, 1865. This was true of Private Matthew Bone.

. . .

IT'S PROBABLE THAT WHITMIRE AND MATTHEW and George Bone knew each other in Jackson County when they were young. Their families lived near each other not far from the village of Nicholson, north of Athens. Whitmire as a young boy moved with his family to Floyd County, Georgia, and then to Cherokee County, Alabama, where he became a farmer.

The Bones left Jackson County as youngsters, moving with their family to Athens in Clarke County. As a young man, Matthew Bone frequently advertised as a house painter also doing ". . . signs, furniture painting, graining and marbleing [sic] of all designs, paper hanging, glazing, & c[ategory]."[19] George Bone was enumerated as a farmer in the 1860 Clarke County federal census.

Captain Grady, their commanding officer, was "well known in Macon County, North Carolina" where many of the Twenty-Fifth Regiment's members lived, according to Augustus Longstreet Hull in his Annals of Athens.[20] Grady was also a prominent businessman in Athens and had many friends in the town, explaining the large number of Clarke County men serving in the Twenty-Fifth North Carolina Infantry. Captain Grady was promoted to major but died in the siege of Petersburg, Virginia, in 1864.[21]

Whitmire's Company "H" was recruited from Cherokee County, Alabama. The Nineteenth Alabama had a proud, long record, taking very heavy casualties at Shiloh and other battles. It finally surrendered in North Carolina on April 26, 1865.[22] John M. Whitmire had three brothers in the same regiment, Joseph, Benjamin F., and Parmenius. Several descendants of John M. Whitmire were especially helpful in collecting family information about the Whitmire family and making it available for this book.[23]

Scattered Records

It is likely there were more than 52 Athens area Confederates who chose Union service over staying in prison, but records are scattered or incomplete. (See Table 2, pp. 44–46, for my listing of the Galvanized Yankees born in Clarke or counties adjacent to Clarke.)

This search was made possible, although incomplete, by combing portions of a huge spreadsheet created by one dedicated individual,

Major Robert Denney (Retired U.S. Army), in the 1990's. Major Denney died of lung cancer soon after his spreadsheet was finished.

"Bob did years of research at the National Archives, constructing a database built on Confederate soldiers' service records, the records of Confederate soldiers in Union prisons and the records of those same soldiers who volunteered to join Union regiments being sent to fight in the Indian wars—the so-called Galvanized Yankees," said his longtime friend, Dr. Tom Lowry. Dr. Lowry, following Major Denney's wishes, has made available the spreadsheet.[24]

To tap its wealth of information, I tried to decode or convert the complex spreadsheet, created in a now-obsolescent computer program. Even with expert help, this was only partially successful, however, producing some quantities of searchable text and locating some Galvanized Yankees born in Clarke and surrounding counties.

These counties during the Civil War were: Clarke, Jackson, Madison, Oglethorpe, Greene, Morgan, and Walton. At that time Oconee and Barrow counties had not been established. Oconee was carved out of the southwest portion of old Clarke County in 1875, and Barrow was created in 1914. Galvanized Yankees were listed as being born in Clarke and all bordering counties existing at the time of the Civil War.

More details about Major Denney's efforts of many years to gather military information about Galvanized Yankees, along with decoding problems, are in the Appendix, page 65.

6   Putting on Blue

Chapter 2

Lincoln's Bright Idea

SOME UNION AND SOUTHERN PRISONS had mortality rates as high as 30 per cent from disease, malnutrition or abuse. Mark Weber, a historian studying Civil War prisons, says "The best and most reliable estimate [of overall mortality] seems to be the one provided by Adjutant General Fred Crayton Ainsworth in 1903. He estimated the mortality rate was about 15.5 per cent in Southern prisons and slightly over 12 per cent in Northern prisons."

Weber, studying Civil War captivity, mentions 30 per cent death rates at some prisons. Weber says while prisoner exchanges between the North and South were common earlier in the war, the exchanges were limited the last two years of the war, adding greatly to overcrowded prisons.[25]

Northern military and political leaders knew the South was hurting for troops even more than the North. It was to the Union's advantage to cut the number of fighting men in Southern armies. But the North had planned for a short war and didn't have the prison capacity necessary to handle the thousands of Confederates who were captured.

As the war dragged on, the Union suffered attrition in its forces, too. Its armies, for example, were short of soldiers to carry out policing the West against increasing Indian attacks, and guarding stage coaches, settlers and the new telegraph lines. President Abraham Lincoln, accompanied by his Secretary of War, Edwin M. Stanton, personally visited the Union military prison at Point Lookout, Maryland, on Dec. 26, 1863.

"He had heard that a significant number of rebel prisoners had expressed willingness to take the oath of allegiance to the United States and swear acceptance of emancipation in return for a full presidential pardon," wrote Doris Kearns Goodwin in her book, *Team of Rivals.* "The general in charge of the prison confirmed this hopeful intelligence when Lincoln and Stanton arrived. . . ."[26]

The President, his cabinet members, other politicians and leading military officers approved helping garrison the West and Upper Middle West, using former Confederate troops. Sending Confederate prisoners would relieve the shortage of federal military men in the West. By sending these Confederate-now-Union troops West, they would not have to fight their former brothers-in-arms. Thus was born the rather strange concept of Galvanized Yankees. They were commanded by professional U.S. Army officers, who, as they saw the former prisoners' service to the Union, generally gave them high marks for their military abilities. In addition to freedom from prison, the Galvanized Yankees received pay, food, clothing and medical care. In some instances, the ex-Confederates received enlistment bounties of $100.[27]

Lincoln had strong political considerations for using ex-Confederates in the Union's military units. As military manpower became scarce, the Northern states were given quotas of men for Civil War service. Lincoln saw the possibility for political support in a presidential election year by meeting draft quotas by substituting ex-Confederates for service.

Pennsylvania and Indiana were two states where Confederate prisoners served as substitutes. An example was George W. Bone's enlistment at Mauch Chunk, Pennsylvania. He was a substitute for one man in its congressional district quota, military records show.

On Dec. 29, 1863, the *New York Tribune* confirmed Lincoln's interest in using ex-Confederate soldiers in the Union forces. "The President and Secretary of War returned to-night from a short visit to the encampment of Rebel prisoners at Point Lookout. It is understood that they satisfied themselves that not less than a thousand, or about a tenth of the whole number, are ready to enter the service of the United States."[28]

The term Galvanized Yankees began as a negative one, but was later assumed by the Confederate prisoners themselves without stigma attached to it—except by Southern patriots and troops who thought it was better for captured Confederates to remain in prison at all costs than to help the Union. When their Union enlistments were completed after the Civil War, apparently many Galvanized Yankees hesitated to return to face possible low opinions of friends and neighbors. Some moved to other counties or states, frequently settling in the West.

Pvt. Lafayette Rogan of the Thirty-Fourth Mississippi Infantry was imprisoned at Rock Island Prison and wrote his strong feelings against those who took the Union loyalty oath in September, 1864. On September 29 he wrote in his diary that several hundred had gone over to the enemy:

"This is the sadest [sic] day of all days of my prison life. 15 men deserted us and take up arms against our cause. Oh how depraved the men of the present generation are become. Self, home, parents, dear wife and children are abandoned for the sake of a few oz [ounces] of meat and bread—God forgive."[29]

Some Galvanized Yankees, however, received a welcome after completion of their service in the Union forces. They returned home to become respected members of various communities. These included Private Whitmire, who returned to Alabama near Mentone. He died there in 1918. His tombstone was a Confederate veteran's marker, honoring his service to the Nineteenth Alabama, but somehow his company was noted as "D" instead of the correct "H" in that unit. He had served in Company "D" in his Union regiment.

Chapter 3

Losing Their War Appetite

ON JULY 3, 1863, the Union was victorious at Gettysburg. And the next day Vicksburg on the Mississippi was captured by Gen. Ulysses S. Grant. It is no wonder that many Southerners—and some Confederate prisoners in Federal prisons—began losing their appetite for the war.

Even a major general of the Confederacy, Patrick R. Cleburne, on Jan. 2, 1864, predicted the South's coming defeat. He read his statement to the staff of Confederate General Joseph Johnston. Four other generals were among those endorsing his opinions, which would be forwarded to Confederate President Jefferson Davis.

"We have now been fighting for nearly three years, have spilled much of our best blood, and lost, consumed or thrown to the flames an amount of property equal in value to the specie currency of the world. Through some lack in our system the fruits of our struggles and sacrifices have invariably slipped away from us and left us nothing but long lists of dead and mangled," General Cleburne's report read.

He pointed out that the Confederacy had already lost more than one-third of its territory to Union soldiers. "Our soldiers can see no end to this state of affairs except in our own exhaustion. . . . They are sinking into a fatal apathy, growing weary of hardships and slaughters which promise no results," he said. He saw "black catastrophe . . . not far ahead of us."[30]

11

General Cleburne had one drastic solution: arming the slaves to fight against the Union. Others began to share this opinion in 1864 and early 1865, but President Davis let the idea die until the very last of the war, when it was too late to try it.

Whitmire Supports Secession Early in War

Early in the Civil War when John M. Whitmire volunteered for the Nineteenth Alabama Infantry Regiment, he wrote in a letter that he ". . . supported secession with all his might," according to a descendant, Glenda M. Patton of Rock Spring, Georgia. "I have a copy of a handwritten letter John wrote from camp in late 1861 in which he was hoping for a fight and spoke of the soldier's life," she wrote. "Many years later in his federal military pension application, he says, in effect, that he was forced into the [Confederate] service."[31]

I wonder whether some Galvanized Yankees might have gotten Confederate service pensions as well as Union military pensions. Although it's a small sample, this writer has found that about 40 per cent of the Galvanized Yankees received U.S. pensions or at least made applications for them. If some served under an assumed name as Galvanized Yankees, it is possible they also obtained Confederate pensions.

A Difficult Choice

It was a difficult choice for Confederate soldiers to become members in Northern military units. But the Bones and Whitmire must have decided the odds were better for keeping alive if they got out of the Northern prisons and headed West in the U.S. Army.

Whitmire was captured at the battle of Missionary Ridge at Chattanooga, Tennessee, on Nov. 25, 1863.[32] At first he refused to take an oath of allegiance to the Union. But finally in late November,

1864, he signed up for one year's service and was put in Company "D" of the Third U.S. Volunteer Infantry Regiment, one of six regiments made up mostly of Galvanized Yankees. Other U.S. regiments also sometimes added ex-Confederates to their ranks.

Whitmire took the U.S. enlistment oath from Union Capt. (later Major) Henry Reed Rathbone, who was entrusted by President Lincoln to interview and recruit possible enlistees at Rock Island and other military prisons.

Captain Rathbone was promoted to Major on March 13, 1865, for gallant and meritorious service in Virginia battles and was a favorite of the President and Mrs. Lincoln.

Rathbone and his fiancèe, Clara, were with the President and Mary Todd Lincoln at Ford's Theatre the night the President was assassinated, dying the morning of April 15, 1865. Major Rathbone had tried to subdue John Wilkes Booth, the assassin, but Booth slashed him severely and escaped.

The Major was obsessed by his failure to save Lincoln. This obsession and self-blame lasted many years, even after he resigned his military rank. Rathbone in the 1880's was living abroad and was appointed U.S. consul general in Hanover, Germany.

"On December 23, 1883, Henry suffered another attack of madness, and went after his children. Clara rushed to defend them, and Henry shot her three times, then stabbed himself five times. Clara died immediately," Frederick Hatch writes in his book, *Protecting President Lincoln*.[33]

Enlisting with Union Forces

Military service records indicate the Bones and Whitmire swore allegiance to the Union and to faithfully serve in its military forces. We have copies of their enlistment papers. (See gallery following page 23.) Military records detail the Union service career of Whitmire (recorded sometimes as Whitmeyer), and we know he served until his Union enlistment term was complete in November, 1865, when honorably discharged. After years of effort Whitmire received his Union military pension, and his widow obtained a widow's pension for his service.[34] Federal bureaucrats at first wanted to deny Galvanized Yankees pensions for their Union service, saying they had not been fighting Confederates. But they were eventually overruled.

Matthew Bone was captured at Petersburg, Virginia, on April 2, 1865, fighting as part of the Twenty-fifth Infantry Regiment of North Carolina.[35] He was imprisoned at Point Lookout and took his oath to the Union there.[36] But no more military records seem available on Bone. It is possible he served under an assumed name, as did many other Confederates becoming Galvanized Yankees. Some Galvanized Yankees also were sent to other military units in the North, but were not tabulated as former Confederates. We have no record that Matthew Bone ever returned to Athens, Georgia.

He leaves few records after he took the enlistment oath at Point Lookout. We do, however, find him and his wife Nancy and two sons living in the small town of Simpsonville, Shelby County, Kentucky, as recorded in the 1870 federal census. He still gave his occupation as a painter. Nancy, listed as a widow in the 1880 census, is found in Lamar County, Alabama, living alone. The census reported her occupation as "farmer." There was no indication she had remarried.

Thus Matthew must have died between 1870 and 1880, although we have no death record. There is no indication Matthew Bone ever filed for a U.S. military pension or for a Confederate service pension.

George W. Bone's life was tragic and short. He fought in the Twenty-Fifth North Carolina Infantry, as part of the Army of Northern Virginia. At the Battle of Malvern Hill, near Richmond, the Confederates suffered more than 5,300 casualties. George Bone was wounded at Malvern Hill on July 1, 1862, according to Confederate military records.[37] He continued his military service despite his wound.

Confederate records for George Bone include information forwarded by Union military officials. On Aug. 30, 1864, George was on a Yankee register "of enlisted men, rebel deserters and refugees detained at Camp Distribution awaiting orders."[38] A rather cryptic note from Northern military information given to the Confederates called George Bone "reb deserter," and indicated he was "released to Baltimore" on Aug. 31, 1864.[39]

George was only confined a few days at Bermuda Hundred, Virginia, which had a Union military prison. On Aug. 30, 1864, a military register from the Provost Marshal indicated he was captured at "Department Headquarters." His record came from Fort Monroe, Virginia, and at some point was sent to his Confederate unit. Another notation concerning George Bone in the prisoner register says "To go north. Oath taken. Reb Deserter." This reveals he did take an oath of allegiance to the North, and thus became a Galvanized Yankee.

George W. Bone also shows up in the U.S. Army "Special Enlistment Categories, 1859–1862."[40]

Surprisingly, his place of residence was listed as Montreal, Canada. He said he was 21 and a laborer, according to the enlistment register. He joined the U.S. Army in Mauch Chunk, Pennsylvania, and was reported as unmarried. He joined the Fifteenth Infantry Regiment, Co. "E."[41] Perhaps George wanted to throw off any investigation as to where he was from by saying he was from Montreal.

George Bone's life was over on Feb. 18, 1866. He died of smallpox serving in the Fifteenth Regiment in Mobile, Alabama. He was only 24 years old, according to death records of the U.S. Adjutant General's office. His home residence was given as Athens, Georgia. He was buried in Mobile's New City Graveyard, which adjoined the Mobile National Cemetery.[42]

George Bone's grave now has a fine marble Union marker in the large Cemetery, where many Confederate and Union troops are interred.[43]

The Bone family in Athens knew George died of smallpox. This is mentioned in the news stories summarizing Mrs. Millie Bones' letter to Robert E. Lee, his response, and the specifics about where her ten sons saw military duty. Nothing indicated George Bone died serving the Union cause.

Private Whitmire Goes Home

Returning to John M. Whitmire, we find he went home in good shape from the Army years. Soon, Whitmire married, had a family and became a solid citizen of DeKalb County, Alabama, next to Cherokee County on the Georgia border. He was a respected farmer. His farm was near Mentone, Alabama, and is now the site of a Boy Scout camp in the mountains there. Both Bone and Whitmire had numerous relatives still living in Jackson or Clarke counties, Georgia, after the war.

Another Georgia Galvanized Yankee was Absalom Jones of Fairplay, Morgan County. Jones, like John M. Whitmire, had a long life and acceptance by his small community after he returned to the South. He saw duty in the Second U.S. Volunteer Infantry Regiment at Fort Rice, Dakota Territory. He would finish his Yankee service with the Fourth U.S. Volunteer Infantry Regiment, which took over duties for the Second U.S. Volunteers.[44] His Confederate career was with the Fourth Texas Infantry Regiment, as confirmed by military records and his Confederate service grave marker in Prospect Methodist Church Cemetery at Fairplay. No mention is made of his Union service. He received a U.S. military pension and died Sept. 14, 1926.

Chapter 4

"Galvanized Confederates," Too

THE CONFEDERATE GOVERNMENT made a small effort to recruit its Yankee captives, freeing them from Southern prisons to do "field service" digging trenches for defenders of Savannah, for example. This, however, didn't work well.

The *Southern Watchman* of Athens, Georgia, reprinted a story, on Jan. 1, 1865, from a Savannah newspaper saying: "I believe a large number of these men are insincere. Several hundred were in the trenches around Savannah during the late siege. An attempt was made by a number of them to escape to the enemy, in which some twenty-five succeeded and six or seven were killed. . . . The symptoms of infidelity to their oaths were so manifest as to justify the disarming and placing under guard of the whole batch. I think our Government had better not put muskets in the hands of such men, or trust many of them at large."[45]

The South couldn't send its Galvanized Yankees to the West, and it didn't work having the Union prisoners go into battle against their Union brothers. Many quickly deserted from the Confederate ranks.

On the other hand, enlisting Confederate prisoners certainly had advantages for the North. These included (1) relieving the shortage of Union troops in the West and Upper Midwest, (2) relieving overcrowded Northern prisons, and (3) sending ex-Confederates out West and not exchanging them, cutting the Confederacy's troop strength.

General U.S. Grant, who at first was opposed to Galvanized Yankees, finally supported the effort because it had real advantages. He wrote to Washington officials explaining his change of mind. "Every man we hold, when released on parole or otherwise, becomes an active soldier against [us] at once either directly or indirectly. If we commence a system of exchange which liberates all prisoners taken, we will have to fight on until the whole South is exterminated. If we hold those caught they amount to no more than dead men. At this particular time to release all rebel prisoners . . . would insure [Gen. William T.] Sherman's defeat and would compromise our safety here."[46]

Chapter 5

Horrible Northern Prison Conditions

TO UNDERSTAND WHY SO MANY Confederates in the North's prisons joined the Union's military forces, it's necessary to see what they were contending with daily as captives.

James F. Rhodes, Pulitzer Prize-winning historian, used what he termed "the best and most reliable estimate" based on federal Adjutant General Fred Crayton Ainsworth's information in 1903. Ainsworth found that the North had captured 214,865 Confederate soldiers. Of this number he estimated that 25,976 died in prisons. The South had 193,743 Union troops captive, and 30,218 of these died in Southern prisons, Ainsworth estimated.[47]

Of the 52 Galvanized Yankees born in Clarke and adjacent counties I located, the largest number—20—were imprisoned in Rock Island, Illinois prison; Camp Douglas prison in Chicago held 15; Point Lookout, Maryland, prison had 10; Camp Chase, Ohio, had 3; Fort Delaware, Delaware, had 1; Alton, Illinois prison had 1; Bermuda Hundred, Virginia, 1; and Camp Morton, Indiana, 1.

At Rock Island, located on an island in the Mississippi River between Illinois and Iowa, 12,049 prisoners were held in the 20 months it operated. We know that 730 were transferred to other prisons; 3,876 were exchanged; and 1,960 died in prison. About 4,000 prisoners became Galvanized Yankees.[48]

Confederate Army Doctor Thomas F. Berry, imprisoned at Rock Island, gives an account of how Galvanized Yankees were lured into volunteering for the Union. Writing for the *Confederate Veteran Magazine* on "Prison Experiences on Rock Island," Dr. Berry said:

"During 1864 there came into the prison a number of workingmen with saws and hatche[t]s and picks and a lot of lumber under heavy guard. All of the prisoners in twelve barracks were moved out. The barracks were now fenced off from the main prison. Next morning at roll call all the prisoners were informed that the United States had determined to open a recruiting office in our prison walls, and that all [who] would like to take the oath and join the United States army would receive $100 bounty and would be moved into the new enclosure. We called it the calf pen. There never was on earth a more barefaced, insulting infamy put up to poor suffering human nature. They were promised abundant rations, no guard duty; they were told that warm, comfortable clothing would be furnished them, and that they would not be required to be sent South, but would be sent out on the frontier to fight the Indians or hold them in check."[49]

While it may be true that lies were told to persuade volunteers to take the loyalty oath to the Union, it is also true that they were indeed enlisted in regiments generally sent out West and they quickly got out of the prison. Indications are that at least some enlistees received $100 bounties.

A Confederate prisoner at Point Lookout told how he calculated the dangers of staying in prison: "Thousands of men were imprisoned and dying rapidly," he said. "Upon my entry, one of the first things I did was ascertain how many men were dying per day, and to calculate when my time would come, should I live to be the last survivor. The calculation showed I had but a brief time to live."[50]

Private Matthew Bone was captured and imprisoned in Point Lookout Prison. He took the oath of allegiance to the Union there.[51] I have found no record mentioning where he was assigned after enlisting. It is possible he went to a regiment with few Galvanized

Yankees, or used an assumed name. Or he might have made his way home, although no records show this to be the case.

Bob Allen, writing for *The Sun Magazine* of the *Baltimore, Maryland, Sun* wrote: "By the end of the Civil War, more than 20,000 prisoners, twice the number it was designed for, were kept in the [Point Lookout] stockade. . . . The mortality rate continued to rise until prisoner deaths were occurring at the rate of 60 to 65 a day. The overall death rate rose to an appalling 25 per cent, overtaking that of the notorious camp at Andersonville [Georgia]."[52]

A Plan to Capture Lincoln

Confederate military leaders gave serious thought to freeing Confederate prisoners at Point Lookout, and using them in a plan to capture President Lincoln and his wife, Mary, at the U.S. Soldiers' Home three miles north of Washington, D. C. Lincoln and his family favored the Home and he spent much of his time there with his family. He rode horseback to and from the White House on many days. Supposedly the President was lightly guarded by a small force, and would be vulnerable to capture.[53] Serious plans were made to capture Point Lookout and use its prisoners for the raid on Washington. Unrealistic planning and indications Union forces knew of the scheme stopped it before it could be tried. It's also obvious that Confederate leaders had little idea of the wretched condition of Confederates imprisoned at Point Lookout.

Fort Delaware Prison, on Pea Patch Island in the Delaware River, had a sinister reputation for scant rations as well as for diseases and maltreatment. One of the Athens area Galvanized Yankees was taken prisoner and placed there, although he was listed in Ahl's Heavy Artillery as doing garrison duty at the prison. The unit did not go West for its military service. As a garrison member at Fort Delaware, this Galvanized Yankee would have come into close contact with Confederate prisoners. Most of the Galvanized Yankees were not placed in close contact with their former Confederate battle comrades.

A prisoner at Fort Delaware, Captain John S. Swann, told of the desperation for food felt by many captives:

"Not long after my arrival I heard a cry 'Rat call! Rat call!' I went out to see what this meant. A number of prisoners were moving and some running up near the partition, over which a sargeant [sic] was standing and presently he began throwing rats down. The prisoners scrambled for the rats like school boys for apples, not but some of the needy prisoners, and the needy were the large majority, would scramble for these rats. Of course but few were lucky enough to get a rat. The rats were cleaned, put in salt water a while and fried. Their flesh was tender and not unpleasant to the taste."[54]

Citizens of the Confederacy learned of the imprisoned Confederate soldiers deciding to swear the oath of allegiance to the enemy government. For instance, a story in the Sept. 12, 1863, issue of the New Orleans *Times-Picayune* discussed early Galvanized Yankees at Fort Delaware:

". . . [A] large number of our prisoners at Fort Delaware have taken the oath and enlisted in the Federal service. The Federals have already, from prisoners who have taken the oath, enlisted two hundred and seventy men in the Third Maryland Cavalry, one hundred and sixty men in a battalion of heavy artillery, and one hundred and fifty in an infantry regiment. To effect these enlistments they circulate all sorts of lies among the prisoners."[55]

One of the lies was that General Robert E. Lee had resigned, the article said.

"When a prisoner agrees to enlist, his name is put down in a book, and he is marched from the main body of the prisoners to another part of the island to join his companions in shame, who live in tents there. He never comes back among his old comrades, for fear, as one of our informants remarked, 'we should cut his d——d throat.' They were jeered and hooted by their late companions as they pass [*sic*] out from them. They are termed 'galvanized Yankees.'"

The article closed by saying: "Our prisoners are dying in Fort Delaware at the rate of twelve a day. Their rations are six crackers a day and spoiled beef."[56]

1. Unidentified Confederates captured and imprisoned at Camp Douglas, Illinois. Many of these prisoners swore loyalty to the Union to gain their freedom and join the Union forces as Galvanized Yankees. COURTESY OF LIBRARY OF CONGRESS.

2. Confederate prisoners were frequently subjected to very painful hanging by their thumbs in Northern prisons, including Fort Delaware, Chase and Johnson's Island prisons. From Joseph Barbiere's *Scraps from the Prison Table*. COURTESY OF GOOGLE BOOKS.

3. A Confederate prisoner invites a Union guard at Point Lookout, Maryland Prison, to a rat dinner. Prisoners were ill-fed and scavenged food wherever they could. This sketch is from the notebook of Confederate prisoner, Pvt. John Jacob Omenhausser. COURTESY OF UNIVERSITY OF MARYLAND SPECIAL COLLECTIONS. PUBLIC DOMAIN.

4. Fort Delaware Prison was a Union prison containing Confederates captured in the Civil War. Some prisoners also served as guards here. COURTESY OF WIKIPEDIA.

5. Some of Morgan's Confederate Raiders imprisoned at Camp Douglas, Illinois, in 1864. They were captured on their famous raid into Indiana and Ohio. COURTESY OF WIKIPEDIA.

6. Confederate captives at Rock Island, Illinois Prison line up for inspection. Union prisons were ill-prepared to handle so many captives, and many men died of disease and suffered shortages of food. THIS PHOTO APPEARED ON SEVERAL INTERNET SITES IN 2015 WITH NO SOURCE GIVEN.

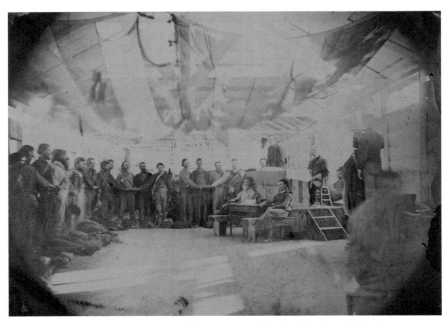

7. Taking the allegiance oath to serve the Union as Galvanized Yankees. This photo was taken at Point Lookout, Maryland Prison. COURTESY OF LIBRARY OF CONGRESS.

8. Confederate Brigadier General M. Jeff Thompson fought in the Trans-Mississippi area of the Confederacy but was captured in 1863 in Arkansas. He was imprisoned in the Fort Delaware prison. He was known as the "Swamp Fox" for his successful fighting abilities. This photo was for his "visiting card" and was taken at Fort Delaware. COURTESY OF WIKIPEDIA COMMONS.

9. This unidentified Confederate prisoner in his tattered uniform and damaged boots was taken at the Point Lookout, Maryland Prison. It is an example of the lack of adequate clothing for many prisoners in Union prisons. COURTESY OF LIBRARY OF CONGRESS.

10. Fort Halleck in Wyoming was the site in 1866 of the murder of Pvt. John R. Cox of Oglethorpe County, Georgia. Cox was shot by a sergeant who alleged Cox, a Galvanized Yankee, had been stealing clothing from a supply facility. Some witnesses said Cox was not stealing. The sergeant was only demoted. COURTESY OF LEGENDSOFAMERICA.COM. PUBLIC DOMAIN.

11. This sketch shows a part of Major General G. M. Dodge's Union regiment traveling between Julesberg, Colorado and Fort Laramie, Wyoming. Galvanized Yankees escorted this unit in this area near Scotts Bluff. COURTESY OF GUTENBERG.ORG.

12. General William T. Sherman, known for his march through Georgia and other states in the Civil War, became head of the Military Division of the Missouri, in charge of U.S. Army activities in the area between the Rockies and the Mississippi River. In 1866, he visited forts where Galvanized Yankees were stationed and labeled some as unfit for human habitation. COURTESY OF LIBRARY OF CONGRESS.

13. This painting by Frederic Remington is entitled "Protecting a Wagon Train"—a frequent job of Galvanized Yankees with military duty in the West. COURTESY OF ATHENAEUM.ORG.

14. Union Army regiments helped protect panic-stricken settlers in Dakota Territory as they fled Indian attacks in 1862. Abraham Lincoln in an address said more than 800 men, women and children were killed in Indian attacks in what is now Minnesota. These settlers were photographed as they fled their homes. Eighty-nine Indians were hanged in one group as a result of their capture. COURTESY OF WIKIMEDIA COMMONS.

15. Spotted Tail's daughter, Ah-Ho-Appa (Fallen Leaf) died in 1866 and asked to be buried on the hillside near Fort Laramie, Wyoming. Sioux and Christian funeral ceremonies were held, and her coffin was placed as pictured here. The garrison at Fort Laramie took part in the funeral. Later, Fallen Leaf was buried at the Rosebud Indian Reservation. COURTESY OF WIKIPEDIA.

16. Cannon guards ruins of Fort Union, near Watrous, New Mexico. The fort was a major military installation on the Santa Fe Trail. During the last two years of the Civil War, numerous Galvanized Yankees were stationed here to protect travelers on the trail. COURTESY OF LIBRARY OF CONGRESS.

17. "Old Bedlam" officers' quarters at Fort Laramie, Wyoming, where many Galvanized Yankees served as the Civil War was ending and Reconstruction began. HISTORIC AMERICAN BUILDINGS SURVEY WYO, 8-FOLA, 1–2. COURTESY OF THE LIBRARY OF CONGRESS.

18. Alfred R. Waud's sketch of cavalry fighting in an 1863 Civil War skirmish as dismounted "Indian style" troops. Frequently Galvanized Yankee units fought in this manner. COURTESY OF LIBRARY OF CONGRESS.

19. Depiction of the Fort Fetterman Massacre in 1866, named for the hapless Capt. William J. Fetterman who led his U.S. Army unit in battle against Indians who killed all 81 of his troops. It was the worst defeat of the Army along the frontier. COURTESY OF WIKIPEDIA.

20. This sketch by a Union Army enlistee shows Fort Laramie in the isolated and barren portion of what is now the State of Wyoming. COURTESY OF THE LIBRARY OF CONGRESS.

21. Brevet Major Enoch G. Adams, commander of a company made up of Galvanized Yankees at Fort Rice, Dakota Territory. In his goodbye to his men, he said: "You will never regret the sacrifice you have made. It will yet be the proudest boast of your life: 'I have been a Union soldier.'"
COURTESY OF DAVID MORIN, THROUGH FINDAGRAVE.COM

22. John M. Whitmire, a Galvanized Yankee veteran in the U.S. Army during the Civil War after he was captured and placed in a Union prison. He took the opportunity to swear allegiance to the Union and enlisted in a Galvanized Yankee regiment. He was born in Jackson County, Georgia, but moved to Alabama. He returned from his Union service and drew a Union pension. COURTESY OF GLENDA M. PATTON.

VOLUNTEER ENLISTMENT.

STATE OF ILLINOIS,

TOWN OF ROCK ISLAND,

I, _John M. Whitmire_ born in _Jackson_ in the State of _Georgia_ aged _Twenty four_ years and by occupation a _Farmer_ Do HEREBY ACKNOWLEDGE to have volunteered this _Fifteenth_ day of October, 1864, to serve as a **SOLDIER** in the **Army of the United States of America,** for the period of _ONE YEAR,_ unless sooner discharged by proper authority: Do also agree to accept such bounty, pay, rations, and clothing, as are, or may be, established by law for volunteers. And I, _J. M. Whitmire_ do solemnly swear, that I will bear true faith and allegiance to the **United States of America,** and that I will serve them honestly and faithfully against all their enemies or opposers whomsoever; and that I will observe and obey the orders of the President of the United States, and the orders of the officers appointed over me, according to the Rules and Articles of War.

Sworn and subscribed to, at Rock Island Barracks this _15_ day of October 1864, _John M. Whitmire_

BEFORE _____

Capt. 12th, U. S. Infantry.

23. Pvt. John M. Whitmire's enlistment record as a Union volunteer and Galvanized Yankee. During his early Confederate service he was very loyal to the South, but when in a Union prison decided to swear loyalty and serve in the Union Army in the West. COURTESY OF THE NATIONAL ARCHIVES.

24. William Ansley, (front row, third from left), veteran of the
    Galvanized Yankees of the Union Army, saw duty in the
    West. Although he had been a loyal Confederate soldier, he
    decided to swear loyalty to the Union and served during
    the Civil War. He was born in Clarke County, Georgia.
    COURTESY OF LESLIE VANDERHIEDE.

25. William H. Ansley of Clarke County, Georgia, enlisted in
    the U.S. Army as a Galvanized Yankee in October, 1864,
    gaining freedom from Rock Island, Illinois Prison. He
    was a farmer and finished his Union service honorably.
    COURTESY OF THE NATIONAL ARCHIVES.

Painting, Painting, Painting!

THE undersigned would announce to the citizens of Athens and vicinity, that he will execute, in the neatest and most workman-like manner, all work in his line of business at short notice. Plain, house, sign and furniture painting, graining and marbleing, of all designs, paper hinging, glazing, &c. Orders from neighboring towns, villages or country, promptly attended to. (Sept 6) MATTHEW BONE.

26. Prior to his military service as a Galvanized Yankee, Matthew Bone was a well known painter who frequently advertised in Athens, Georgia, newspapers. Although he did not return to Athens, the 1870 census for Simpsonville, Kentucky, indicates he was a painter there after the Civil War. THIS AD APPEARED IN THE OCT. 18, 1860 ISSUE OF *THE SOUTHERN WATCHMAN*.

27. The Oath of Allegiance to the Union, sworn by Matthew Bone of Clarke County, Georgia. See the bottom of the oath certificate which gives his name as Matthew Bone. He was a Confederate soldier captured and then imprisoned at Point Lookout, Maryland. He and his wife lived in Kentucky after his military service for the U.S. Army. COURTESY OF THE NATIONAL ARCHIVES.

28. George W. Bone was a Galvanized Yankee who served in the U.S. Army's Fifteenth Infantry in the last years of the Civil War. His Mobile, Alabama, National Cemetery marker indicates he was from Pennsylvania, but that was where he enlisted after being captured as a Confederate soldier. He died of smallpox in Mobile. COURTESY OF "G-MAN" THROUGH FINDAGRAVE.

29. The U.S. Navy ship Onondaga, barely above water-level, was where Jackson County, Georgia, Galvanized Yankee John C. Widener saw a portion of his Union service. This photograph shows the Onondaga on the James River in Virginia. COURTESY OF THE NATIONAL ARCHIVES.

30. Enlistment Record of Pvt. Absalom Jones of Fairplay, Morgan County, GA. He swore loyalty to the Union and agreed to serve for three years in a regiment of Galvanized Yankees. COURTESY OF THE NATIONAL ARCHIVES.

31. Henry Harrison Lancaster of western Jackson County, Georgia, was captured by Union soldiers and imprisoned in Camp Douglas, Illinois Prison. He served as a Corporal in the Fifth U.S. Volunteer Infantry as a Galvanized Yankee. COURTESY OF RICHARD MAYOR.

32. This Union military marker of Henry Harrison Lancaster is the only ex-Confederate from the Athens area the author found who received a Union marker. He is buried in Sterling Cemetery, Sterling, Oklahoma. COURTESY OF DARREL A. RONSHAUSEN.

33. Galvanized Yankee John Bledsoe Harper, with beard, was from either Morgan or Walton County. He returned home after his service in the Second U.S. Volunteer Infantry. His second wife, seated, is Texanna Levi Tidwell. COURTESY OF RON JONES.

34. The honorable discharge of John R. Cox of Oglethorpe County, Georgia. The Army felt it necessary to give him this discharge after he had been murdered by a sergeant at Fort Halleck in Wyoming. He was a mechanic and worked in the supply section as a Galvanized Yankee. COURTESY OF THE NATIONAL ARCHIVES.

35. This U.S. Navy ship, the steamer Circassian, was one of the duty stations of "Galvanized Tar" Henry Clay Gilbert who enlisted in the U.S. Navy. Gilbert was one of two Jackson County, Georgia, ex-Confederates to enlist in the U.S. Navy. COURTESY OF NAVAL HERITAGE AND HISTORY COMMAND.

36. A Confederate marker indicates the service of Henry Clay Gilbert of Jackson County, Georgia, before he took the oath of allegiance to serve in the Galvanized Yankees. He is buried in the Pendergrass Baptist Church Cemetery. COURTESY OF PENNY K. STOWE.

37. Painter John Gast's "American Progress" or "Westward the Course of Destiny." This is a chromolithograph done in 1873. The print shows an allegorical female figure representing America leading pioneers, using various kinds of transportation as they head West. The Galvanized Yankee Union soldiers played a major role escorting and protecting these settlers against Indians. COURTESY OF LIBRARY OF CONGRESS.

38. In this William Henry Jackson painting the artist shows settlers crowding the Platte River Bridge in central Wyoming. The U.S. Army installation by the bridge was involved in many battles during and immediately after the Civil War with Indian tribes. THIS COPY IS IN PUBLIC DOMAIN.

39. Fort Rice, Dakota Territory, where many Galvanized Yankees were sent to help the Union Army protect pioneers, guard trails and control Indian skirmishes. During the Civil War, Fort Rice was a much simpler installation. Painting done by Seth Eastman in 1871. COURTESY OF WIKI MEDIA.

ASSASSINATION OF PRESIDENT LINCOLN.

40. Major Harry Rathbone tries to stop John Wilkes Booth from shooting President Lincoln at Ford's Theater. With him is his fiancee, Clara Harris, left and Mary Todd Lincoln, Lincoln's wife. Rathbone was a special friend of Lincoln and was active in enlisting Galvanized Yankees at Northern Prisons. He enlisted several Athens area Galvanized Yankees and signed their enlistment papers. Lithograph by H. H. Lloyd & Co. COURTESY OF LIBRARY OF CONGRESS.

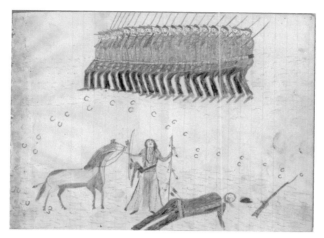

41. A Kiowa warrior celebrates the death of a U.S. soldier while a mass of soldiers is in the background. Note the two arrows in the dead soldier. COURTESY OF NEWBERRY LIBRARY SPECIAL COLLECTIONS.

42. "The Siege of New Ulm" by Henry August Schwabe. This depicts the battle between Dakota braves and settlers in 1862. The battle took place during the Dakota Wars when the Indians, defrauded of lands, money and supplies, struck at the Minnesota town. This caused an evacuation of about 2,000 settlers to Mankato, Minnesota, escorted by 150 troops. Some sources indicate 500 settlers and 100 soldiers were killed. Nearly 40 Indians were hanged, but battles continued for 30 more years. COURTESY OF WIKIPEDIA.ORG.

43. Kiowa Chief Hawgone or Silver Horn (c. 1860–1940). He was known as one of the most talented Kiowa artists, depicting subjects such as traditional activities, Sun dances, warfare and everyday life. He sketched with crayon, pen and ink and other materials on paper ledger paper and on muslin. Galvanized Yankees in the West frequently tried to prevent or punish Kiowa depredations. This portrait was by E. A. Burbank. COURTESY OF WIKIPEDIA.

44. Fort Leavenworth National Cemetery at Fort Leavenworth, Kansas, was used as a burial place as early as the 1840's, but was officially established in 1862. Many of the burials there were of military enlisted men and officers stationed on the frontier in Arizona, Colorado, New Mexico and Wyoming. More than 22,000 graves are there. Some Galvanized Yankee ex-Confederates are among the dead. COURTESY OF WIKIPEDIA.

The Room in the McLean House, at Appomattox C. H., in which GEN. LEE surrendered to GEN. GRANT.

45. Surrender of Gen. Robert E. Lee to Gen. U. S. Grant, April 9, 1865, at Appomattox, Virginia. COURTESY OF WIKI ADMINISTRATION.

Chapter 6

Western Frontier Service

EX-CONFEDERATES FROM CLARKE COUNTY and the surrounding area served in all six of the regiments established for Galvanized Yankees, mainly in the West's frontier areas, including what we now call the upper Midwest. (A few from Northeast Georgia enlisted in other Union military units.)

Seven of the men were assigned to the First U.S. Volunteer Infantry Regiment, the first Galvanized Yankee regiment organized. It enlisted captives at Point Lookout Prison between January and March, 1864. After a brief period when the regiment saw duty around Norfolk, Virginia, the unit was split in its move west. Four companies went to the Minnesota-Dakota frontier. The remaining six companies were sent to construct and man Fort Rice, situated on the Upper Missouri River in Dakota Territory.[57]

Eleven Athens area men ended up in the Second U.S. Volunteer Infantry Regiment. Five were placed in the Third U.S. Volunteer Regiment. These regiments were approved by President Lincoln in September, 1864, when he okayed 1,750 more Galvanized Yankees for the Second and Third U.S. Volunteer Regiments. He did this to improve his presidential election chances, mainly in Pennsylvania, against Gen. George B. McClellan.[58] The men could substitute for men in the quota for conscription into Union forces.

The Second U.S. Volunteer Infantry Regiment saw duty guarding the Santa Fe Trail in Kansas and also the new Butterfield stagecoach route there. They also served in Colorado Territory in and around Fort Lyon. Companies also were garrisoned at Forts Larned, Riley, Scott, and Zarah, all in Kansas; and at Fort Dodge in Iowa.

Duty stations for the Third U.S. Volunteers included Kansas, Nebraska, and Colorado and Idaho territories.

Assignments for the Fourth U.S. Volunteers included Forts Rice, Berthold, Sully and Randall, all in Dakota Territory.

The Fifth U.S. Volunteers were active at Fort Riley, Kansas, guarding the Santa Fe Trail; Fort Leavenworth, Kansas; Fort Halleck, Idaho Territory; and Denver, Fort Lyon, Camp Wardell, and Fort Collins, all in Colorado Territory; Fort John Buford in Wyoming; and in several Montana locations.

The Sixth U.S. Volunteers served in Fort Leavenworth, and along the Oregon Trail; and at Fort Rankin, and Fort Laramie, Wyoming. The regiment also saw varied short-term duty in quite a few posts in the Territory of Nebraska and Idaho Territory.

Five Athens area Confederates ended up in the Fourth U.S. Volunteer Infantry, which was authorized in October, 1864, but didn't get into the field until February, 1865.

Twelve Confederate recruits from the Athens area were placed in the Fifth U.S. V., which began to see duty in the West in spring, 1865. The Sixth U.S. V. contained five Athens area Galvanized Yankees, plus one soldier who also served in the First U.S. V. It was organized on April 2, 1865. Two Athens area ex-Confederates were placed in Ahl's Independent Heavy Artillery Battalion [Delaware Heavy Artillery] for duty at Fort Delaware, Delaware.

Two Athens area Galvanized Yankees served in the U.S. Navy and one in the Fifteenth U.S. Volunteer Infantry. The Union service unit for two men from Athens and adjacent counties could not be determined.

A scattering of Galvanized Yankees served in other Union military units. They included The Third Maryland Cavalry, Eleventh Ohio Cavalry; and the First Connecticut Cavalry. Some troops from these units had duty in the West or Upper Midwest. As far as I could determine, no Athens, Georgia, area Galvanized Yankees were assigned to these units.

George W. Bone, one brother of Matthew Bone, was a Galvanized Yankee who did serve in a unit apart from the First through the Sixth U.S. Volunteer Infantry Regiments. He took the oath of loyalty to enlist in the Fifteenth U.S. Infantry Regiment.[59]

What Happened to Galvanized Yankees?

We can see with some certainty what the Galvanized Yankees' duties were in the First through Sixth U.S. Volunteer regiments. Monthly post returns indicated activities of their units. It isn't possible to consider half-a-hundred Galvanized Yankees from the Athens area in detail, but we can recount the military service of a few who are especially interesting.

See Table 2, pp. 45–46, which gives descriptions of 52 Athens area Galvanized Yankees, their Confederate Units and Galvanized Yankee Regiments. Table 3, pp. 47–48, gives their counties of enlistment and their occupations.

Ex-Confederates serving in the Union forces in the West had no bed of roses. The post returns, or reports, made monthly to the Adjutant General in Washington, testify to their hardships.[60] Galvanized Yankees died, some violently as they fought Indians. In one battle against mainly the Sioux Indians, the Third U.S. Volunteer Infantry Regiment suffered 25 deaths at the Battle of Platte River Bridge in Wyoming. An estimated 3,000 Indians made a huge attack on the small 120-man garrison and the nearby bridge across the Platte. I have not found any records of deaths of Athens area Galvanized Yankees in this battle. The Indians were finally beaten off after they suffered heavy losses.

Weather extremes in the West were fierce, and Southerners were unused to 30-below zero temperatures and blizzards. Post barracks were frequently ill-constructed, but at least there was a roof over their heads and a guaranteed place to sleep and food to eat. Boredom was frequently a problem with dull routines, but at least there were chances for excitement and action.

Eventually Army officers came to accept the ex-Confederates. In the main, they did not desert at a higher rate than regular troops, and their fighting abilities were good. Discussing Galvanized Yankees, Capt. Enoch Adams, a Fort Rice Company "D" commander, First U.S. Volunteer Infantry, said: "Many have laid down their lives at the beck of disease; some have been murdered by the arrow of the [Indian], and but few exceptions, living or dead, have been true to their trust."[61]

Pvt. John M. Whitmire

Ex-Confederate John M. Whitmire of Jackson County, Georgia, had a rather typical military service for frontier-based troops, regimental records indicate. He enlisted Oct. 15, 1864, for about one year with Company "D" of the Third U.S. Volunteer Infantry. Whitmire was 24 years old and stood 5 feet 11 inches tall.[62] As a Union private he was assigned to Post Cottonwood, in Nebraska Territory. This post later became Fort McPherson.

He was kept busy building military buildings, escorting settlers moving to the Upper Midwest and probably had some skirmishes with Indians. Whitmire enlisted for only one year, as did other Third U.S. V. Regiment members.[63]

Whitmire began duty at Post Cottonwood on May 7, 1865. He soon was placed on detached service to smaller posts or camps. These included Enestein, Miller's Station and Mullally's Station. He returned to Post Cottonwood for September and October. He was mustered out with an honorable discharge on Nov. 29, 1865.[64] His records point out that he had never been paid in full, nor had he received his clothing account. It was little more than a year since John M. Whitmire had been taken prisoner at the battle of Missionary Ridge at Chattanooga, Tennessee.

Soon Whitmire was on his way home and returned to Alabama in late 1865. Two years later he married Mary Isabelle Hamilton. They lived for 12 years in Tennessee, and then moved back to Alabama. He died at Mentone, DeKalb County, Alabama, on May 6, 1918, being 77 years old.

His tombstone has his company designation incorrect on the Confederate marker for his service in the Nineteenth Alabama. It incorrectly indicates he was in "Company "D" of that Regiment. "D" was his company in the Third U.S. Volunteer Infantry, a Galvanized Yankee Union regiment. He was in Company "H" in the 19th Alabama.[65]

Cpl. William P. Conner

Cpl. William P. Conner, a Clarke County, Georgia, farmer, enlisted on March 15, 1862, in Company "F" of the Infantry Battalion of Cobb's Legion of Georgia Volunteers. Howell Cobb of Athens commanded the Infantry brigade of the Legion, and recruitments were made throughout the state. In 1860, according to the federal census, the Conner family was living near Flint Hill in Carroll County, Georgia, having moved from Clarke County.

In 1850, a William L. Conner was enumerated in the federal census as being 18 years old, a farmer, and living with the family of John S. Wright, in Puryear's District of Clarke County, Georgia. This Conner may have been the Confederate soldier Conner.

On June 4, 1864, Cobb's Legion records indicated he was absent, being "missing, killed or captured." He gave his birthplace as Clarke County in Union military records.[66] He was captured at Gaines Mill, Virginia, on June 2 and sent to Point Lookout Prison in Maryland on June 8.

Before the month was out, on June 27, 1864, he swore allegiance to the Union and enlisted in Company "F" of the First U.S. Volunteer Regiment.[67] By November, 1864, Conner had been promoted to corporal, a rare occurrence for Galvanized Yankees. He was placed on duty in the Quartermaster Department. His regiment was sent to the Districts of Dakota and Minnesota, and also ordered to build and garrison Fort Fletcher [later Fort Hays], Kansas. The regiment's duties also included guarding the new Butterfield Stage route.

Cpl. Conner was involved in one of the largest battles in the West when Sioux Indians surrounded Fort Rice in Dakota Territory. The Sioux were protesting loss of their hunting grounds and rotten meat issued to them by the federal government. Three U.S. Volunteer Regiment enlisted men died in the battle. The troops successfully broke the Fort Rice encirclement, killing and wounding a large number of Indians.

Disease, however, was a much greater cause of death among the troops at Fort Rice. Scurvy was a leading cause of death.

Writing a letter, William D. Vencil, an enlisted man in the First U.S. Volunteers, described what Fort Rice was like: "We are in one of the worst country in the world [at] the present time we have to fight indians every few Days we have been here 9[?] months and we have lost 78 or 79 men out of the Regt most Died of disease we have only lost 4 or five killed by Indians."[68]

In November, 1865, Conner's company was on detached service escorting travelers from Fort Fletcher, Kansas, to Monument Station, Kansas. Also in November the regiment chased Indians committing depredations along the Butterfield Stage route, according to post returns of Fort Fletcher.

The Indians were engaged on November 24 at Downers Station. Troops killed seven and wounded a number of others.

The next day, Indians attacked two stages escorted by First U.S. Volunteer Regiment troops. "Five Indians were killed," the record of events on the Fort Fletcher regimental return reported.

Conner mustered-out from the Union Army on May 10, 1866, nearly a year after the war was over. He received a Union invalid's pension, and after his death his widow received a widow's pension.[69]

Chapter 7

Navy Men—Two "Galvanized Tars"

WHEN THE GALVANIZED YANKEES PROJECT was set up, one of the first suggestions made to President Lincoln was placing ex-Confederates in the U.S. Navy, where there would be fewer of their ex-compatriots to battle. Naval service, however, didn't seem popular with most ex-Confederate prisoners, and emphasis shifted to sending the Galvanized Yankees West.[70] There were, however, some Galvanized Yankee sailors, military records show. These included Henry Clay Gilbert and John C. Widener, both of Jackson County, Georgia.

This county contributed a large number of Galvanized Yankees, and was the birthplace of the two "Galvanized Tars," Gilbert and Widener, according to Civil War records in Major Denney's spreadsheet and U.S. Navy archives of the Civil War.[71] The families of both men had lived for decades early in the Nineteenth Century in Jackson County. Gilbert and Widener lived in the same Sub-District 45 of the county, which contributed several other Galvanized Yankees to the Union forces.

Henry Gilbert was born about 1840, according to the 1850 Jackson County federal census, and was a farm laborer. In 1861 he enlisted as a private in Company "C" in the Georgia Eighteenth Infantry Regiment. He was wounded and captured near Nashville, Tennessee, on Dec. 3, 1863, and placed in the Rock Island, Illinois, military prison. Gilbert took the oath of allegiance to the U.S.

government and enlisted in the U.S. Navy. He began his Navy service as a Landsman at a Naval Rendezvous at Camp Douglas, Chicago, on Jan. 25, 1864.[72] He saw sea duty on the U.S. S. Circassian. This was a supply ship for the Union's East and West Gulf Blockading Squadrons.[73] Gilbert received a Navy pension for his service, and his widow also had a Navy pension[74]

A John J. Widener was enumerated in the 1850 U.S. non-population census of Jackson County as farming 20 acres of improved land and having an additional 30 acres of unimproved land. Value of his farm was estimated at $130. He may have been the father or a relative of John C. Widener. John C. Widener was not in the 1850 or 1860 federal censuses for Jackson County.

Widener served as a private in Company "E," Eighth Arkansas Infantry, enlisting on Sept. 10, 1861.[75] Among his various assignments was ordnance duty, and his occupation was gunsmith. He served at the Selma, Alabama, Arsenal.[76] The records also state that Widener became a prisoner of war when captured November 25, 1863, at Missionary Ridge, Tennessee. He was sent to Rock Island, Illinois Prison on Dec. 9, 1863.[77] The Roll of Prisoners indicated Widener enlisted in the U.S. Navy at Rock Island and transferred to Camp Douglas, Illinois, thus making him a Galvanized Yankee.

Major Denney's Galvanized Yankee spreadsheet indicates Widener had the rank of Landsman for the Navy in Chicago, as had Henry C. Gilbert.[78] A Landsman was the lowest ranking person in the Navy, having completed less than one year of duty before becoming a Seaman or other rank.

His Navy experience also included service on the U.S.S. Onondaga.[79] This was a shallow-draft Monitor-type vessel with armor-plating. The Onondaga was part of the James River, Virginia, Flotilla, covering water approaches to Richmond.

Widener became a Third Class Fireman as he advanced in the Navy. Another assignment took him aboard the historic U.S.S. North Carolina, whose service began in 1820. The ship sailed throughout the world. It had 74 guns and was a three-masted square rigger.[80]

During the Civil War the ship was a receiving ship for training in the New York Navy Yard. It was sold for scrap in 1867.[81]

Navy records indicate that Widener was also crew member on the Union ship Kensington which helped win the First Battle of Sabine Pass in Texas, lobbing shells into a Confederate installation in a blockade of the Texas coast. Confederates, however, did win another definite victory later at Sabine Pass.

Widener ended his active Navy career and received an invalid's pension. His widow also was awarded a pension for his Naval service.

Chapter 8

A Well-Kept Secret

OF THE GALVANIZED YANKEES FROM CLARKE and surrounding counties whose burial sites I have located, only one has his Union military service recorded on his tombstone. The others I have located have Confederate military markers. The exception is Henry H. Lancaster, born in Jackson County. He died in Oklahoma and lies under a Union military marker there.

Lancaster was the son of John and Laura Lancaster, who in 1860 were living in the J. Randolph District near the Mulberry post office in western Jackson County. Henry was 16 in 1860 and was listed as a "farm laborer" in the Jackson County, 1860 census.

Lancaster enlisted as a private in Company "D" of the 55th Georgia Infantry Regiment on May 12, 1862. This regiment fought in East Tennessee, and on Sept. 11, 1863, Henry was wounded and then captured by Union forces at Cumberland Gap. He was imprisoned at Camp Douglas, Illinois, where he remained until several days after General Lee surrendered at Appomattox. On April 15, 1865, he swore loyalty to the federal government and joined the Fifth U.S. Volunteer Infantry. He was sent West to Fort Leavenworth, the Union's oldest installation in the West and a base for its efforts to guard settlers and trails and combat Indians.

Lancaster must have made a good soldier in his Union outfit. He was promoted to corporal before he was mustered out at Fort

Leavenworth on Nov. 13, 1866, long after the war was finished. His unit was one of the last ones disbanded as a Galvanized Yankee force.

The Jackson County native was rewarded with an invalid pension given to him by the federal government. After his death, his wife Sinthiean [Cynthia Ann], received a widow's pension.

In the later years of their lives they had moved to the Indian Territory. Lancaster died in October, 1919, according to the application for a U.S. military headstone, requested by Wiley N. Kelly. It was sent to Kelly's rural home 13 years later and placed on Lancaster's grave. Its inscription reads "Corporal, Company 'I', 5 Regt. U.S. Vol." It is a tall marker in Sterling Cemetery, Comanche County, Oklahoma, indicating that he had been a loyal soldier to the Union. The marble marker was carved in Columbus, Mississippi, and shipped to Oklahoma on Aug. 20, 1932.

All the other Galvanized Yankees for whom I have located military markers have their Confederate service and unit designation on their tombstones. Perhaps Lancaster or his relatives felt he had moved to a part of the country which would not think badly of this ex-Confederate who became a Galvanized Yankee.

Murder of Pvt. John R. Cox[e]

A number of Galvanized Yankees died fighting Indians or from disease, but I found one from the Athens area who was murdered out West. This was Pvt. John R. Cox (some military records add an "e") who was born in Oglethorpe County. His murder is described in records of the Fifth U.S. Volunteer Infantry where he served.

Private Cox enlisted in Company "E," Forty-Third Georgia "Rebel" Infantry, as Union military records indicate. He was captured after the Battle of Resaca, Georgia, May 13–15, 1864.[82] At Resaca, Gen. William T. Sherman flanked Confederate General Joseph Johnston, forcing him to withdraw toward Atlanta.

Cox was a 29-year-old mechanic or machinist, standing 5 feet 10 inches tall.[83] In the 1850 federal census of Oglethorpe County, John

Cox, 17, was living in the county, and was the son of Frances Cox. In the 1860 census for Elberton in Elbert County, adjoining Oglethorpe County, we find a J. R. Coxe, mechanic, who is apparently the same man as in the 1850 Oglethorpe census.

After his capture, Cox was placed in the Alton, Illinois, military prison. He took the oath of allegiance to the Union and was placed in Company "A" of the Fifth U.S. Volunteer Infantry Regiment. The Fifth U.S.V. was the next-to-last of the six Galvanized Yankee regiments to be formed. One of the main jobs for the regiment was guarding the Overland Trail and Santa Fe Trail, furnishing escorts and drivers for stage coaches and wagons.

The Georgia native was assigned to quartermaster supply duty for the companies of the regiment stationed at Fort Halleck, Dakota Territory in what is now the state of Wyoming.[84]

As I browsed through the post returns for the Fifth U.S. Volunteer Regiment companies sent to Fort Halleck, in the "Loss," section I found the surprising notation: "John R. Cox . . . killed by Sergt. S. Hertz 5th U.S. Vols Jany 18th 1866."

In the service file of Private Cox, quoting from the post return for the month of January, 1866, we find under remarks: "Killed by Sergt. S. Hertz, Co. E. 5th U.S. Vols., Jany 18, 1866."[85] In a "Final Statement of John R. Cox" is the brief quotation "Murdered Jany 18th 1866.[86]" In Union military units, a "Final Statement" was an accounting of a soldier's death and its causes.

Solomon Hertz (Army records also list his name as Hurtz or Hurst) enlisted as a private at Columbus, Ohio, April 21, 1865. He was born in New Orleans, Louisiana, and was listed variously as a 20-year-old laborer or miner in 1865 documents. He enlisted with the Fifth U.S. Volunteers for three years as a Galvanized Yankee.[87] There is some confusion about which Confederate unit he belonged to before taking the Union oath. One service card indicates he served in the Thirteenth Louisiana Infantry, being promoted from private to corporal, but no date of enlistment is given.[88] Hertz also went by the name of Joseph G. Hurst when he enlisted in the Fifth U.S. Volunteers.[89] He was promoted to sergeant on May 14, 1865, as a duty clerk in the adjutant's office of the Fifth U.S. V. He was shown as acting sergeant major for a battalion and then put in charge of the quartermaster's clothing store, Fort Halleck post returns indicate.[90]

After the death of Cox, on Feb. 1, 1866, Hertz was "absent in arrest at Camp Collins, C. T." (Colorado Territory). He continued to Denver City, C. T., still under arrest. Hertz alleged he shot Cox for stealing from the clothing store at Fort Halleck, but some witnesses disagreed.[91] He was charged with murder by Army officials.

But by June, 1866, Hertz was back on daily duty in the Fort Halleck adjutant's office as clerk. He was mustered out of the service on Oct. 11, 1866, at Fort Kearny, Nebraska Territory, as a private. Apparently his punishment for the murder was his loss of his sergeant's stripes. There is no indication he was tried by court martial.

Following Army rules, Cox had to be mustered out, even though he was dead. This was done at Fort Kearny on Oct. 11, 1866.[92] The "Remarks" section on the mustering-out roll said: "Died at Ft. Halleck D. T.[Dakota Territory] Jany. 18, '66 from the effects of a gun shot."

His company commander, Capt. R. G. Butler, signed a certificate with Cox's mustering-out papers, which ended with the words: ". . . having served HONESTLY and FAITHFULLY with his company to the present date, is now entitled to a **DISCHARGE** [sic] by reason of Murder."

An inventory of Cox's effects included "1 great coat, 1 blouse, 1 pair of cotton drawers, 1 pair of boots, 1 pair socks, 2 woolen blankets, 1 rubber blanket, 1 revolver and belt, and 1 breach pin."[93]

Fort Halleck was de-activated on July 4, 1866, as there was little reason to keep it operating as use of the Overland Trail dwindled. Company "F" of the Fifth U.S. Volunteers remained at Fort Halleck to guard government property.

There are no entries in Fort Halleck post records that any relatives ever attempted to claim the personal effects of Private Cox or to take custody of his body for burial. He was probably buried in the Fort Halleck post cemetery, although no records show this.

James R. Pittard

James R. Pittard was born in Clarke County, according to the Denney Galvanized Yankee spreadsheet. He was a member of a well known family. James D. Pittard was an early mayor and commissioner of Athens, Georgia, and Pittards had been in the county before 1850.

James R. Pittard was a laborer, and became a Confederate private in 1861 in Captain Swett's Light Artillery in Mississippi. He was promoted to corporal in that unit or its successor. He was captured near Nashville, Tennessee, and made a prisoner in 1865 at the Alton, Illinois, prison.

At Alton he took the oath to become a Galvanized Yankee, enlisting in the Fifth U.S. Volunteer Infantry Regiment on May 2, 1865.[94] This regiment soon saw service in the West. A few weeks after General Lee surrendered, the Fifth was sent to Fort Leavenworth, Kansas. By May, 1865, companies of the Fifth were stationed at various forts in the West to guard movement along the Santa Fe trail against Indian attacks.

Private Pittard "lucked-out," because his Company "B" was sent to Denver to carry out quartermaster duties, Denver probably being a better assignment. He saw duty at Fort Kearny, Nebraska, as well. He had also been an orderly for a Captain McDougall at Fort Laramie, Dakota Territory, now Wyoming state.[95]

The Fifth U.S. Volunteer Infantry was one of the last Galvanized Yankee regiments to be discharged. Finally Gen. William T. Sherman closed Fort Lyon, where the Fifth was in service, because Sherman termed it "unfit for human habitation."[96] This ended the duty of the last companies of the Fifth as Galvanized Yankees. These men were mustered out on Nov. 13, 1866. Twenty-five-year-old Pittard was discharged a month earlier, saying goodbye to the Union Army on Oct. 11, 1866.

A J. R. Pittard, born in Georgia, is shown as living in Clarke County, Mississippi, in the 1860 federal census. This probably was the Galvanized Yankee born in Clarke County, Georgia. U.S. Army pension records showed that he applied for a pension due him for his services with the Fifth U.S. Volunteers. The pension index indicates he applied, but doesn't show final approval or disapproval. Pittard was part of the household of James H. Pittard listed in the 1860 census for Clarke County, Mississippi.

(See Table 4, pp. 49–51, indicating which Galvanized Yankees from the Athens area were granted Union military pensions.)

Chapter 9

A Summing Up

MY ESTIMATE OF THE NUMBER of Galvanized Yankees is approximately 7,000 to 8,000, based upon a count of the service records of men in each of the six regiments. This figure subtracts possible "shrinkage" due to duplication of service records. This estimate also subtracts Regular Army officers and non-Galvanized Yankee enlisted men.[97] There were probably hundreds of Galvanized Yankees serving in other Union military units, having sworn the oath of allegiance to the Union, but harder to trace. My conservative estimate includes about 1,000 Galvanized Yankees serving in Union Regiments other than the First through Sixth U.S. Volunteer Regiments.

For example, ex-Confederates served in the First Connecticut Cavalry, the Third Maryland Volunteer Cavalry, the Third Pennsylvania Heavy Artillery Volunteers, the Fourth Delaware Infantry, the Eleventh Ohio Cavalry Volunteers, and Ahl's Heavy Artillery Company at Fort Delaware, according to several authorities. Clarke County, Georgia, Galvanized Yankee George W. Bone enlisted in the U.S. Fifteenth Infantry Regiment.

The fact that so many Confederate troops swore allegiance to the Union may show the Confederate soldiers' increasing despondency about the turn the Civil War had taken. If the South had been winning the war, probably fewer of its soldiers would have enlisted as Galvanized Yankees. By joining their former enemies, they were freed from hellish prisons and had a chance to serve in the West, where they would not have to kill their former Confederate compatriots. While disease was still a major killer of Union troops, and Indians posed a significant danger, Galvanized Yankees obviously preferred to take their chances outside prisons.

The total number of Galvanized Yankees I found who were born in Clarke and adjacent counties probably doesn't thoroughly show the extent of the transfer of allegiance. Access to the complete research of Robert Denney, would undoubtedly add many to the list of those joining the Union side from Northeast Georgia.

The military records we have show most of these Galvanized Yankees were farmers, but not owners of large plantations. Few were from families holding many slaves. Nearly all were privates in their Confederate units and may not have identified strongly with plantation and slave owners in the South's military service. The men may have doubted the myth of the romantic South—the South of chivalry, moonlight and magnolias.

Some of the local Galvanized Yankees moved on to make a new start in other areas after the Civil War, choosing not to return to their previous homes in the South. Some did return, however, and resumed living where they were born and raised. The men who became Galvanized Yankees had to grapple with the moral issues of their decision to join the Union army. It was a decision each man had to make on his own.

It is likely that those who returned to communities where they were known before the war were frequently not happily accepted as Galvanized Yankees.

A Goodbye to the Galvanized Yankees

Capt. Enoch G. Adams, from Durham, New Hampshire, and a company commander at Fort Rice, Dakota Territory, wrote his goodbye to his Galvanized Yankees in the last issue of *The Frontier Scout* newspaper there. He was a Regular U.S. Army officer:

"We are the first fruits of a re-united people. We are a link between the North and the South—let us prove that it is a golden link, and south, east or west, let us bear the flame of liberty in our hearts. . . .

"You have passed through scenes of suffering; believe that the All-Merciful has something good in store for you. . . . Soldiers, I love you. I am a soldier, and have been for nearly five years. In almost every grade from the lowest, I have served, and tried to do my duty. I do not regret the sacrifice. And you will never regret the sacrifice you have made. It will yet be the proudest boast of your life: 'I have been a Union soldier.'"[98]

On April 24, 1869, Captain Adams was made a Brevet Major for "gallant and meritorious service during the war." He received this promotion for his leadership in the First U.S. Volunteer Infantry, with the Galvanized Yankees.[99]

TABLE 1
The Bone Family's Sons as Military Members
During Civil War and Mexican War

NAME OF SOLDIER	DATE OF BIRTH	RESIDENCE	ENLISTMENT DATE	MILITARY UNIT
Bone, Clark[e] Pvt.	1844	Athens, GA	Feb 1, 1864	Lumpkin Artillery (Confederate)
Bone, George W. Pvt.	1838	Athens, GA	July 8, 1861	"G" 25th Regt. Inf. NC (Confederate)
Bone, George W. Pvt.*	1838	Athens, GA	Oct. 21, 1864	15th U.S. Volunteer Inf. (Union)
Bone, Hardeman Pvt.	1818	Forsyth County, GA	?	12th Georgia Cavalry (Confederate)
Bone, James. Pvt.	1825	Athens, GA	1861 [?]	23rd GA Battalion, GA Volunteers (Confederate)
Bone, Jonathan Pvt.	1820	Jackson County, GA	Mar. 21, 1862	"G" 25th Regt. Inf. NC (Confederate)
Bone, Joseph Pvt.	1845	Athens, GA	May 2, 1862	Troup Artillery (Confederate)
Bone, Matthew Pvt.	1833	Athens, GA	Apr. 20, 1862	"G" 25th Regt. Inf. NC (Confederate)
Bone, Matthew Pvt.*	1833	Athens, GA	June 24, 1865	Took enlistment at Pt. Lookout Prison (Union)
Bone, Sanders Pvt.*	1824	Athens & Macon, GA	May, 1847	13th Regt Inf. U.S. Army (Mex. War)
Bone, William M. Pvt.	1835	Athens, GA	Apr. 29, 1861	Athens Guards (Confederate)
Bone, Willis C. Pvt.	1843	Athens, GA	Apr. 29, 1861	Athens Guards (Confederate)

*Both George W. Bone and his brother Matthew Bone swore allegiance to the Union and served in Union units, as well as in their original Confederate units. George served in the 15th U.S. Volunteer Infantry, and Matthew took the loyalty oath to the Union, but we don't know his specific unit, other than it was a unit not in the 1st through the 6th U.S. Volunteer Infantry Units. George died of smallpox while serving with the 15th USV in the occupation of Mobile, AL. Sanders Bone served in the Mexican War, but I have not found any record that he served in the Civil War.

TABLE 2
Athens Area Galvanized Yankees
and Their Confederate and Union Regiments

NAME	CONFEDERATE UNIT	UNION UNIT
Agan, John F.	23rd Georgia Inf.	4th USV
Allen, John W.	1st Regt. GA State Troops	4th USV
Ansley, William H.	?	2nd USV
Baker, Benjamin H.	4th Regt. Alabama Inf.	4th USV
Bone, George W.	25th NC Volunteer Inf.	15th U.S. Inf.
Bone, Matthew	25th NC Volunteer Inf.	?
Brew[y]er, Benjamin P.	5th Georgia Inf.	2nd USV
Caldwell, Robert L.	6th Inf. GA [?]	1st USV
Carlisle [Carlile], Green	21st Georgia Inf.	?
Carter, James M.	?	1st USV
Conner, William P.	Cobb's Legion, Inf. Bn.	1st USV
Cox[e], John R.	43rd GA Inf. Regt.	5th USV
Ellison, David	1st Confederate Inf.	3rd USV
Gann, Marion	3rd Georgia Cavalry	5th USV
Gilbert, Henry C.	18th Georgia Inf.	U.S. Navy
Glover, John S.	15th Georgia Inf.	2nd USV
Harper, John	18th Alabama Inf.	2nd USV
Herring, David	?	4th USV
Hogan, John	16th Georgia Inf.	2nd USV
Humphries, Marcus T.	30th Georgia Inf. [?]	3rd USV
Johnson, John M.	?	6th USV
Jones, Absalom R.	4th Texas Inf.	4th USV
Kil[l]gore, Henry S.	3rd Georgia Inf.	5th USV
Lancaster, Henry H.	55th Georgia Inf.	5th USV
Landers, John B.	Cobb's Legion, Cav. Bn.	2nd USV
McEver, Joseph	?	5th USV
Mann, Reuben J.	8th Georgia Inf.	2nd USV
Nelson, George W.	19th Louisiana Inf.	3rd USV
Osborn[e], John H.	111th Alabama Inf.	2nd USV

TABLE 2
Athens Area Galvanized Yankees
and Their Confederate and Union Regiments *(continued)*

NAME	CONFEDERATE UNIT	UNION UNIT
Pittard, James R.	?	5th USV
Poage, Robert H.	2nd Regt. Georgia Volunteers	lst USV
Preston, Thomas C.	9th Mississippi Inf.	2nd USV
Rhodes, Lafayette	30th Mississippi Inf.[?]	6th USV
Ridley, William	3rd Tenn. Mtd. Inf.	6th USV
Roberts, John T.	13th Georgia Cavalry	5th USV
Robertson, John W.	12th Georgia Inf.	6th USV
Rooks, [Roots?] John W.	141st Georgia Inf.	2nd USV
Smith, Marion F.	?	Del. Hvy. Arty.
Smith, Mial [Miles] C.	13th Georgia Cavalry	5th USV
Spencer, Patrick J.	Cobb's Legion, Inf. Bn.	5th USV
Spruell, John W.	13th Georgia Inf.	1st USV
Stamps, James J.	38th Georgia Inf.	1st USV
Stewart, John H.	1st Confederate Inf.	5th USV
Westbrooks, Doctor M.	34th Georgia Inf.	5th USV
Wheeler, Willis	40th Georgia Inf.	Del. Heavy Arty.
Whitmire, John M.	19th Alabama Inf.	3rd USV
Whitten, Berry A.	56th Georgia Inf.	2nd USV
Widener, John C.	8th Arkansas Inf.	U.S. Navy
Williams, Levi W.	13th Georgia Cavalry	5th USV
Wood, William P [T.?].	27th Georgia Inf.	3rd USV
Wooten, John T.	56th Georgia Inf.	1st & 6th USV
Wooton, William S.	26th Georgia Inf.	6th USV

46 *Tables*

TABLE 3
Athens Area Galvanized Yankees,
Their Counties and Occupations

NAME	COUNTY	CIVILIAN OCCUPATION
Ansley, William W.	Clarke	Farmer
Conner, William P.	Clarke	Farmer
Gann, Marion	Clarke	Farmer
Humphries, Marcus T.	Clarke	Farmer
Landers, John B.	Clarke	Farmer
Pittard, James R.	Clarke	Laborer
Poage, Robert H.	Clarke	Farmer
Spencer, Patrick J.	Clarke	Farmer
Wheeler, Willis	Clarke	Cooper
Wood, William P.	Clarke	Farmer
Caldwell, Robert L.	Greene	Artist
Rhodes, Lafayette	Greene	Farmer
Agan, John F.	Jackson	Farmer
Bone, George W.	Jackson	Farmer
Bone, Matthew	Jackson	Painter
Carlisle, Green	Jackson	Laborer
Ellison, David	Jackson	Farmer
Gilbert, Henry C.	Jackson	Farmer
Herring, David	Jackson	Carpenter
Johnson, John M.	Jackson	Farmer
Lancaster, Henry H.	Jackson	Farmer
McEver, Joseph	Jackson	Blacksmith
Ridley, William	Jackson	Farmer
Roberts, John T.	Jackson	Farmer
Smith, Marion F.	Jackson	Farmer
Spruell, John W.	Jackson	Mechanic
Westbrooks, Doctor M.	Jackson	Engineer
Whitmire, John M.	Jackson	Farmer
Widener, John C.	Jackson	Blacksmith

TABLE 3
Athens Area Galvanized Yankees,
Their Counties and Occupations *(continued)*

NAME	COUNTY	CIVILIAN OCCUPATION
Williams, Levi W.	Jackson	Farmer
Glover, John S.	Madison	Farmer
Osborn, John H.	Madison	Student
Harper, John	Morgan	Farmer
Jones, Absalom R.	Morgan	Farmer
Mann, Reuben J.	Morgan	Farmer
Robertson, John*	Morgan or Hart*	Farmer
Rooks, John W.	Morgan	Farmer
Whitten, Berry A.	Morgan	Farmer
Wooten, John T.	Morgan	Farmer
Wooton, William S.	Morgan	Farmer
Cox[e], John R.	Oglethorpe	Machinist
Stamps, James J.	Oglethorpe	Farmer
Allen, John W.	Walton	Laborer
Baker, Benjamin H.	Walton	Engineer
Brewer, Benjamin P.	Walton	Farmer
Carter, James M.	Walton	Cooper
Hogan, John	Walton	Farmer
Kil[l]gore, Henry S.	Walton	Farmer
Nelson, George W.	Walton	Farmer
Preston, Thomas C.	Walton	Farmer
Smith, Mial [Miles] C.	Walton	Farmer
Stewart, John H.	Walton	Carpenter
*Sources on County Vary		

TABLE 4
Athens Area Galvanized Yankees Receiving Union Military Pensions

NAME	RANK	COUNTY	INVALID PENSIONS	DEPENDENTS PENSIONS
Agan, John F.	Pvt.	Jackson	Yes: #447292	Yes: #554723
Allen, John W.	Pvt.	Walton	No	Yes: #719010
Ansley, William H.	Pvt.	Clarke	No	Yes: #782146
Baker, Benjamin H.	Pvt.-Sgt.	Walton	Application: #491007	
Bone, George W.	Pvt.	Clarke	No	
Bone, Matthew	Pvt.	Clarke	No	
Brew[y]er, Benjamin P.	Pvt.	Walton	No	
Caldwell, Robert L.	Pvt.	Greene	No	
Carlisle, Green	Pvt.	Jackson	No	
Carter, James M.	Pvt.	Walton	Yes: #636375	Yes: #580485
Conner, William P.	Pvt.-Cpl.	Clarke	Yes: #1072.645	Yes: #942283
Cox[e], John R.	Pvt.	Oglethorpe	No	
Ellison, David	Pvt.	Jackson	Yes: #1108358[?]	
Gann, Marion	Pvt.	Clarke	No	
Gilbert, Henry C. (Navy)	Landsman	Jackson	Yes: #20217 Navy	
Glover, John S.	Pvt.	Madison	No	
Harper, John	Pvt.	Walton	No	

TABLE 4
Athens Area Galvanized Yankees Receiving Union Military Pensions *(continued)*

NAME	RANK	COUNTY	INVALID PENSIONS	DEPENDENTS PENSIONS
Herring, David H.	Pvt.	Morgan	Yes: #455809	Yes: #960.857
Hogan, John	Pvt.	Morgan	No	
Humphries, Marcus T.	Pvt.	Clarke	Yes: #1093830	
Johnson, John M.	Pvt.	Jackson	No	
Jones, Absalom	Pvt.	Morgan	Yes: #547585	
Killgore, Henry S.	Pvt.	Walton	No	
Lancaster, Henry H.	Pvt.	Jackson	Yes: #1270360	Yes: #710869
Landers, John B.	Pvt.	Clarke	Yes: #478124	Yes: #710869
Mann, Reuben J.	Pvt.	Morgan	No	
McEver, Joseph	Pvt.	Jackson	No	
Nelson, George W.	Pvt.	Walton	Yes: #1162476	
Osborn, John H.	Pvt.	Madison	No	
Pittard, James R.	Pvt.	Clarke	Application #1159951	
Poage, Robert H.	Cpl.	Clarke	No	
Preston, Thomas C.	Pvt.	Walton	Yes: #392960	
Rhodes, Lafayette	Pvt.	Greene	No	
Ridley, William	Sgt.	Jackson	No	

TABLE 4
Athens Area Galvanized Yankees Receiving Union Military Pensions *(continued)*

NAME	RANK	COUNTY	INVALID PENSIONS	DEPENDENTS PENSIONS
Roberts, John T.	Pvt.	Jackson	No	
Robertson, John W.	Pvt.	Morgan	No	
Rook[s], John W.	Pvt.	Morgan	Application #1105658	Yes: #366407
Smith, Marion F.	Pvt.	Jackson	No—died in service	Yes: #353.222
Smith, Mial [Miles]	?	Walton	No	
Spencer, Patrick J.	Pvt.	Clarke	No	
Spruell, John W.	Pvt.	Jackson	No	
Stamps, James J.	Cpl.	Oglethorpe	Yes: #1076957	
Stewart, John H.	?	Walton	No	
Westbrooks, Doctor M.	Pvt.	Jackson	Yes: #1047019	
Wheeler, Willis	Pvt.	Clarke	Yes: #565175[?]	Application: #968958
Whitmire, John M.	Pvt.	Jackson	Yes: #1087178	Yes: #857.433
Whitten, Berry A.	Pvt.	Morgan	Yes: #1112672	Yes: #743.209
Widener, John C. (Navy)	Fireman	Jackson	Yes: Navy #15798	Yes: Minors Navy Cert. #21020
Williams, Levi W.	Pvt.	Jackson	No	
Wood, William P.	Pvt.	Clarke	No	
Wooten, John T.	Pvt.	Morgan	No	
Wooton, William S.	Pvt.	Morgan	No	

About the Endnotes

With information utilized from the Internet, problems in citing sources become intensified. Internet sites are often quickly outdated, or the site vanishes and can't be found. Studies have shown that within a few months or a year, a large percentage of websites are obsolete or missing. Also, a web footnote or endnote can become too ridiculously long to be practical. Appending the "access date" when giving a website address citation tells us nothing except it was in existence on a specific date. Saying a site was available Jan. 1, 2014, for example, does not guarantee anyone will ever find it again.

. . .

A large amount of the information in this book comes from military records, which are often difficult to understand and sometimes hard to find. Hundreds of millions have been digitized, which is very helpful, but are not necessarily easy to use. Some are available free and others are found through subscription services, such as Fold3.com or Ancestry.com.

Many military records are archived by the National Archives and Records Administration (NARA), in Washington, D.C., or at other locations. Some state and local archives are also sometimes placed online.

Citing the web "frame" address pertaining to an individual soldier's record will not give the file on the individual soldier. Although I am an "all access" subscriber to Fold3.com, it is first necessary to type the soldier's name into the program to start my search for more information. If the name is found, the searcher is presented with many possible servicemen having the same name. A rather long and sometimes confusing "narrowing-down" process is necessary. The searcher must select from among dozens or sometimes hundreds of persons with the same name. Then when the correct person in the correct military unit is located, it is necessary to go through dozens of documents in the individual's military service record to find the facts needed, such as the date of enlistment, rank, type of service, time of mustering-out, or leaving the service, and whether the soldier (or sailor) received a pension for his service.

Service records were originally filed in jackets for each person. These service record entries, however, are not in chronological order. Bits and pieces are scattered here and there in the soldier's overall service record and its digital copy, or elsewhere, as in reports by the Adjutant General, or in records of prisoner-of-war facilities. It is helpful before using Fold3.com to know the specific war period, along with the name of the specific military unit to which the soldier belonged. The person searching doesn't always know these things.

Digitized source information obviously should come from original or authoritative sources. Many original military records are housed at the NARA in Washington, D. C. or elsewhere, or in state archives. These records may be in original format or may be microfilmed copies. They are usually the closest we can get to many original military records.

In this book, I have chosen to give the NARA source of such information rather than use cumbersome web address citations. The endnotes give as precise a location of information as possible, but the user may still have to do extensive searches, using NARA headings or catalogs. These are often found with the digitized online information.

Some sources cited are not available anywhere else but on a website. I believe the reader expects to know where the original pre-digitized material is housed and made available whenever it is possible. When such information has originated on the web, I do cite its web address.

As online digital sources proliferate, researchers or curious readers may decide which ones they prefer to use. The endnotes in this book furnish information citing the original sources or copies in respected archives whenever possible.

U.S. federal census information used in this book is not endnoted, as the census digitized sources are so readily available. The census year and location of the specific enumeration are given in the body of the text.

Abbreviations and Definitions

NARA: National Archives and Records Administration, Washington, D.C.

Microfilm Identifications: An example: M1017 is the microfilm publication of the service records of the First through the Sixth U.S. Volunteer Regiments of Galvanized Yankees. Some records begin with a "T" instead of an "M" and aren't as much in demand by the public. Some microfilm sources also utilize alphabetical listings, such as military pension records. Finally each type of file belongs to its own Record Group. In these endnotes a citation will first give the microfilm publication name, then the specific roll number and finally the Record Group to which the material belongs.

Cav.: Cavalry

Co.: Co. "A" means Company A of a larger unit, such as a regiment or battalion.

Bn.: Battalion.

Inf.: Infantry.

Mtd.: Mounted, as in Third Volunteer Mtd. Regiment.

Regt. or Reg't.: Regiment.

U.S.V. Inf. Regt.: U.S. Volunteer Infantry Regiment.

Abbreviations for various ranks: Pvt. for Private; Cpl. for Corporal, Sgt. for Sergeant; 2nd Lt. for Second Lieutenant; 1st Lt. for First Lieutenant; Capt. for Captain; Maj. for Major; Lt. Col. for Lieutenant Colonel; Col. for Colonel and Gen. for General.

Bvt.: Brevet, placed in front of a specific rank, such as Bvt. Major. Such an officer has the rank of major, but may not continue to hold it permanently or have the pay or privileges of the rank. The brevet or commission to the officer was frequently given for outstanding or meritorious service. Often officers who had been brevetted in war conditions saw their rank reduced in a smaller peacetime army.

Endnotes

1. NARA M1017. Roll 33. Record Group 94. "Compiled service records of former Confederate soldiers (Galvanized Yankees) who served in the 1st through 6th U.S. Volunteer Infantry Regiments, 1864–1866." Military Unit: 3d U.S. Volunteers, We-Z.

2. NARA M233. Roll 77. Record Group 94. "Registers of Enlistments in the United States Army, 1798–1914." (Special Enlistment Categories, Duplicates, p. 77.) George W. Bone.

3. NARA M270. Roll 313. Record Group 109. "Compiled service records of Confederate soldiers from North Carolina units, labeled with each soldier's name, rank, and unit, with links to revealing documents about each soldier." George W. Bone.

4. The National Park Service, U.S. Dept. of the Interior, Jefferson National Expansion Memorial, "The Galvanized Yankee," *The Museum Gazette*, July, 1992 issue. http://www.nps.gov/jeff/historyculture/upload/galvanized__yankees.pdf. This article points out that few prisoners were being exchanged by 1863 and prisoners were left in captivity in ". . . horrible, filthy places which lacked all the basic necessities of life." Prisoners could expect to remain in prison until the end of the war—if they lived.

5. The National Park Service, "The Galvanized Yankee," In *Museum Gazette*, above. See also Dee Brown's book *The Galvanized Yankees* (Lincoln and London: University of Nebraska Press, 1986), for the best all-around history of this group. The National Park Services' "The Civil War" indicates there were 462,634 Confederate troops imprisoned in the Union's prisons. Of this number 247,769 were "paroled in the field." That would leave 214,865 not paroled. After doing a census of men serving in six regiments mainly made up of "Galvanized Yankees," and cutting out duplicate service records for the same man, I calculated at least 3.5 per cent of the ex-Confederates in Yankee prisons chose to enlist in the Union forces, to be sent West. See also http://www.nps.gov/civilwar/facts.htm

6. Samuel Bowles, publisher of the Springfield, Massachusetts, *Republican* newspaper was an early user of the term "Galvanized Yankees." He wrote in the *Republican* on June 3, 1865: "Among the present limited number of troops on the Plains are two regiments of infantry, all from the rebel army. They have cheerfully enlisted into the federal service. . . . They are known in the army as 'white-washed rebs,' or as they call themselves, 'galvanized Yankees.'"

7. "Brave Soldiers," *Athens Banner*, Athens, Georgia, May 10, 1895, p. 2.

8. NARA A1158. Roll 1. Records Group 15. "War of 1812 Pension Files, #24827." James Bone. Digitized in Fold3.com project with NARA.

9. Sanders Bone's pension for service in the Mexican War is recorded NARA A1158. Roll 1. "Pensions indexed by number for Army or Navy service in the Civil War and later, 1860–1934," Roll 1, Pension 350, indicating Sanders Bone's pension. Pensions for wars other than the Civil War were also included.

10. Mrs. Bone's letter to General Lee and his reply were published in a long article, running in various newspapers throughout the country. On May 8, 1895, on page 3 of the Atlanta, Georgia, *Constitution*, headlined the article: "Brave Boys Went from Clarke County to the War. General Lee's Letter to the Mother." *Hull's Annals of Athens, 1801–1901*, Augustus Longstreet Hull (Athens: Banner Job Office, 1906) reprinted by Mary B. Warren, 1978, pp. 253–54, also mentions Mrs. Bone's letter to Gen. Robert E. Lee and his reply.

11. The letter and its history was also carried in the May 15, 1895, issue of the *New York Times*.

12. Robert Scott Davis, *Records of Clarke County Georgia, 1801–1892, in the Georgia Department of Archives and History*, (Greenville, SC: Southern Historical Press, 1993), p. 91.

13. John F. Stegeman, *These Men She Gave: Civil War Diary of Athens, Georgia* (Athens: Univ. of Georgia Press 1964), p. 153.

14. The Confederate records of John M. Whitmire (sometimes listed as Whitmeyer) are in NARA M311. Roll 276. "Compiled service records of Confederate soldiers from Alabama Units, Labeled with Each Soldier's Name, Rank, and Unit, with Links to Revealing Documents about Each Soldier." Military Unit: Nineteenth Infantry, Company "H". See also NARA T289. "Pension applications for service in the U.S. Army between 1861 and 1900, grouped according to the units in which the veterans served." Whitmire, John M.

15. NARA M347. Roll 32. "Unfiled Papers and Slips Belonging in Confederate Compiled Service Records.," George W. Bone.

16. NARA, "Final Statements of Deceased Soldiers of the U.S. Infantry During and After the Civil War. Textual Records, the Adjutant General's Office, (1821 to 04-28-1904)," Record Group 94, National Archives Identifier 654719. File of George W. Bone.

17. NARA M270. Roll 313. Record Group 109. "Compiled Service Records of Confederate Soldiers from North Carolina Units, Labeled with Each Soldier's Name, Rank, and Unit, with Links to Revealing Documents about Each Soldier."

18. Frank Cunningham, *General Watie's Confederate Indians* (Norman: Univ. of Oklahoma Press, 1998), p. 198.

19. See advertisement "Painting, Painting, Painting!" in the *Southern Watchman*, Athens, GA, Oct. 18, 1860, p. 3.

20. *Annals of Athens, Georgia, 1801–1901*, p. 239.

21. Ibid., pp. 297–98.

22. "19th Alabama Infantry Regiment History," at www.19thalabama.org.

23. A profile of John M. Whitmire by his great-great granddaughter, Glenda M. Patton, is included in ancestry.com's "stories" in the general listing of information for Whitmire. This is found in the compilation about "John M. Whitmire, Jackson County, GA."

24. Letters and materials sent to the author from Thomas P. Lowry, M. D., during the period from January through the summer of 2014.

25. Mark Weber, "The Civil War Concentration Camps," *The Journal of Historical Review*, Summer 1981 Vol. 2, No. 2, p. 137.

26. (New York: Simon & Shuster Paperbacks, 2006), p. 594.

27. An example of a Confederate prisoner receiving a $100 bounty for one year of service to the Third U.S. Volunteer Infantry Regiment was John F. Abel of Tennessee. Upon swearing his oath of allegiance to the Union at Rock Island Prison he was paid his bonus. Credit for his enlistment was given to the quota of the town of Clarion, PA, 20th Congressional District, to help it meet its quota of men to serve in the Civil War. NARA M1017. Roll 25. Record Group 94. 3d U.S. Volunteers, John F. Abel.

28. "Visit to Point Lookout," p. 4.

29. Weber, p. 137.

30. U.S. War Department (Washington, D. C.: Government Printing Office, 1880–1891), *The War of the Rebellion: A Compilation of the Official Records of the Union and Confederate Armies*, Series 1, Vol. 52 (Part II), pp. 586-7.

31. Email to Al Hester from Glenda Patton, Feb. 24, 2014.

32. NARA M311. Alabama. Roll 276. Record Group 109. "Nineteenth Infantry, John M. Whitmire. Compiled service records of Confederate soldiers from Alabama units."

33. (Jefferson, NC.: McFarland & Co., 2010), p. 161.

34. NARA, Publication T289. Roll 679. "Pension applications for service in the

U.S. Army between 1861 and 1900, grouped according to the units in which the veterans served. Civil War pensions, Volunteers, Regiment 3, Co 'D.' Whitmire, John M."

35. NARA M270. Roll 313. Record Group 109. "Compiled service records of Confederate soldiers from North Carolina units, labeled with each soldier's name, rank and unit, with links to revealing documents about each soldier." Matthew Bone, Twenty-fifth Infantry.

36. Ibid.

37. NARA M270. Roll 313. Record Group 109. Twenty-Fifth Infantry, George W. Bone.

38. Ibid., p. 18.

39. Ibid.

40. NARA M233. Roll 77. Record Group 109. "Registers of Enlistments in the United States Army, 1798–1914," p. 71.

41. Ibid.

42. NARA, Record Group 94. "Final statements of deceased soldiers of the U.S. Infantry during and after the Civil War." Digitized from NARA textual records. Bone, George W. Arm of Service: Infantry; Regiment: 15; Company: E. Death Date: 18-Feb-1866. Adjutant General's Office, March 10, 1866.

43. www.findagrave.com. Grave listing for George W. Bone, Mobile National Cemetery, Mobile, Alabama. This burial listing is imported from U.S. Veterans Affairs data, Find A Grave Memorial #2943372.

44. NARA M1017. Roll 36. Record Group 94. "Compiled service records of former Confederate soldiers (Galvanized Yankees) who served in the 1st through 6th U.S. Volunteer Infantry Regiments, 1864–1866." Absalom R. Jones.

45. "The Siege and Fall of Savannah," p. 2

46. Weber, p. 137.

47. *History of the Civil War, 1861–1865* (New York: Ungar, 1961).

48. Weber, p. 137.

49. Vol. XX, No. 2, February, 1912, p. 66.

50. Bob Allen, "Point Lookout: Andersonville North," *Baltimore Sun Magazine*, April 28, 1974, p. 18.

51. NARA M270. Roll 313. Record Group 109. "Compiled service records of Confederate soldiers from North Carolina units, labeled with each soldier's name, rank, and unit, with links to revealing documents about each soldier." Twenty-Fifth Infantry, Matthew Bone.

52. April 28, 1974, pp. 22–23.

53. http://www.defense.gov/specials/heroes/history1.html. "History of the U.S. Soldiers' and Airmen's Home (USSAH) Washington, D. C."

54. "John Swann's Story—Prison Life at Fort Delaware" on the following website: http://www.censusdiggins.com/fort_delaware.html.

55. "Escape of Confederate Prisoners from Fort Delaware," New Orleans Times-Picayune, Sept. 12, 1863, p. 2.

56. Ibid.

57. Michele T. Butts, "Trading Gray for Blue: Ex-Confederates Hold the Upper Missouri for the Union," Prologue Magazine, National Archives, Winter 2005, Vol. 37, No. 4, has a thorough discussion of the First U.S. Volunteer Infantry Regiment, the initial regiment organized specifically for Galvanized Yankees.

58. Dee Brown, The Galvanized Yankees, (Urbana: University of Illinois Press, 1963); Reprinted as a Bison Book, (Lincoln and London: University of Nebraska Press, 1986), pp. 11–14.

59. NARA Publication M665. Roll 164. Record Group 94. Bone, George W. "Returns from Regular Army Regiments, June 1821–December 1916."

60. To find activities of the Galvanized Yankee regiments, it is first necessary to look up the names of individuals and ascertain the military installations where they saw duty. NARA M1017 usually contains this. Ancestry.com and NARA have jointly digitized the military post returns. Using Ancestry.com to find individual Athens area Galvanized Yankees, military returns listing where they served are usually made available. Then the selected returns may be inspected. Then an investigation of each month's activities recorded on the returns will be necessary for the time period of the individual soldier's duty at the specific installation. NARA M617. makes available "Returns from U.S. Military Posts, 1800–1916" and is the basis of these digitized post returns.

61. National Park Service, Jefferson National Expansion Memorial, "The Galvanized Yankees," The Museum Gazette, July, 1992. www.nps.gov/jeff/historyculture/upload/galvanized_yankees.pdf

62. NARA M1017. Roll 33. Record Group 94. "John M. Whitmeyer [Whitmire], Compiled service records of former Confederate soldiers (Galvanized Yankees) who served in the 1st through 6th U.S. Volunteer Infantry Regiments, 1864–1866."

63. Ibid.

64. See "U.S. Returns from Military Posts, 1806–1916, Nebraska, Cottonwood, Sept., 1863 through Dec., 1865," digitized by Ancestry. com. See individual post listings, first by state or territory and then specific posts. NARA M617, original source for returns. Mainly Record Group 94.

65. Email Feb. 24, 2014, from Glenda Patton, descendant of John M. Whitmire to Al Hester.

66. Company Descriptive Book, Co. "F" First U.S. Volunteer Regiment, lists Clarke County, GA as birthplace for William P. Conner, NARA M1017. Roll 3. Record Group 94. "Compiled service records of former Confederate soldiers (Galvanized Yankees) who served in the 1st through 6th U.S. Volunteer Regiments, 1864–1866, 1st U.S. Volunteers, William P. Conner."

67. NARA M1017. Roll 3. Record Group 94. "Compiled Service Records of Former Confederate Soldiers who Served in the 1st through 6th U.S. Volunteer Infantry Regiments, 1864–1866, Volunteer Enlistment." William P. Conner, June 27, 1864.

68. Letter from William D. Vencil, "Looking Back: the Civil War in Tennessee," from the Tennessee State Library & Archives. See Google's "Tennessee State Library & Archives William D. Vencil."

69. NARA T289. Roll 679. "Pension applications for service in the U.S. Army between 1861 and 1900, grouped according to the units in which the veterans served." Volunteers, Regiment 1, Co. "F," Conner, William P.

70. Dee Brown, *The Galvanized Yankees*, p. 65.

71. Robert Denney Spreadsheet items 12111–12112 pertain to Henry C. Gilbert's Union Navy service. Items 16058 through 16061 refer to John C. Widener's Union Navy service. NARA M1279. "Approved pension applications of widows and other dependents of U.S. Navy veterans who served between 1861 and 1910" John C. Widener, Certificate #21020. NARA M1469. "Case files of Approved Pension Applications of Civil War and Later Navy Veterans (Navy Survivors' Certificates), 1861–1910." Henry C. Gilbert, Certificate #20217. The term "Tars" is an old Navy slang term for sailor. Terry Foenander, an Australian researcher in American Civil War history, used this term for ex-Confederate soldiers who were captured, put in Northern prisons and then given a chance to serve in the Union Army or Navy. See TNGENWEB-L Archives online in a document entitled "American Civil War Galvanized Tars."

72. Lillian Henderson, *Roster of the Confederate Soldiers of Georgia 1861–1865*, V. 2 (Hapeville, Georgia: Longino & Porter, Inc., no date), p. 638.

73. Department of the Navy, "Circassian," *Dictionary of American Naval Fighting Ships*, (Washington, D. C.: Naval History & Heritage Command). The Circassian was an "iron-screw" steamer ship.

74. NARA M1469. Arranged alphabetically. Record Group 15. "Case files of approved pension applications of Civil War and later Navy veterans (Navy Survivors' Certificates), 1861–1910." File of Henry C. Gilbert.

75. NARA M317. Roll 107. Record Group 109. "Compiled service records of Confederate soldiers from Arkansas units, labeled with each soldier's name, rank, and unit, with links to revealing documents about each soldier." Eighth Infantry, John C. Widener.

76. Ibid., "Company Muster Roll," Dec. 31, 1862 to Feb. 28, 1863.

77. Ibid., "Roll of Prisoners of War," showing John C. Widener was imprisoned at Rock Island Barracks, Illinois, Jan. 1, 1864.

78. From Galvanized Yankee spreadsheet by Denney, data on John C. Widener are on Rows 16058-16061.

79. NARA M1279. Record Group 15. "Approved pension applications of widows and other dependents of U.S. Navy veterans who served between 1861 and 1910." Widener, John C. Certificate 21020.

80. Ibid.

81. See http://www.battleshipnc.com/AbouttheShip/History/AllShips.

82. Cox "gave himself up" according to Union Army information furnished to Cox's Confederate regiment. He was listed as captured on May 17, 1864, after the Battle of Resaca, near Calhoun, Georgia, May 15–17. He was imprisoned at the Alton, Illinois Military Prison and enlisted in the Fifth U.S. Volunteer Infantry. NARA M266. Roll 461. Record Group 109. "Compiled service records of Confederate soldiers from Georgia units, labeled with each soldier's name, rank, and unit, with links to revealing documents about each soldier." Forty-Third Infantry. John R. Cox. See also John R. Coxe, "Muster and Descriptive Roll of a Detachment of 5th U.S. Vols. Forwarded for the 5 Reg't U.S. Volunteers" NARA M1017. "Compiled service records of former Confederate soldiers (Galvanized Yankees) who served in the 1st through 6th U.S. Volunteer Infantry Regiments, 1864–1866." 5th U.S. Volunteers, John R Coxe.

83. NARA M1017. Roll 42, Record Group 94. "John R. Coxe, Muster and Descriptive Roll of a Detachment of U.S. Vols. forwarded for the 5 Reg't U.S. Volunteers, March 22, 1865."

84. NARA M1017. Roll 42. Record Group 94. "Co 'C' Company Muster Roll, Nov. and Dec. 1865. Jno. R. Coxe. (Galvanized Yankees)."

85. NARA M1017. Roll 42. Record Group 94. "Company 'C' Return 5. U.S.V., Fort Halleck, Dak. Ter." John R. Cox.

86. NARA M1017. Roll 42. Record Group 94. "Final Statement, John R. Cox, Co. A 5th Reg't of United States Infty Volunteers," Murdered January 18th 1866.

87. NARA M1017. Roll 45. Record Group 94. "Soloman [sic] Hurtz Muster and Descriptive Roll of a Detachment of U.S. Vols. forwarded for the 5th Reg't U.S. Vols. Roll dated Alton Ills May 2 1865," 5th U.S. Volunteers, Solomon Hurtz.

88. NARA M320. Roll 248. Record Group 109. "Compiled service records of Confederate soldiers from Louisiana units, labeled with each soldier's name, rank, and unit, with links to revealing documents about each soldier." Solomon Hurtz.

89. NARA M1017. Roll 45. Record Group 94. Hurst enlisted in the Fifth U.S. Volunteer Infantry, beginning his time as a Galvanized Yankee, released from Alton, Illinois military prison on March 16, 1865.

90. NARA M1017. Roll 45. Record Group 94. "Solomon Hertz, Sgt., Co. E, 5

Reg't U.S. Vol. Inf." A long list of "remarks" including his appointment in charge of the post clothing store, then "absent in arrest" at Camp Collins, C. T. [Colorado Territory], then "absent in arrest in Denver City, C. T. in February, 1866. In June to September, 1866, Hertz [Hurtz] was back on daily duty in the Adjutants' office, as clerk.

91. NARA M1017. Roll 42. Record Group 94. Letter to Capt. J. L. Carpenter, Acting Adjutant General, Fort Halleck, Dakota Territory, Jan. 18, 1866. The letter said that Sgt. Solomon Hertz "states that he caught Cox stealing clothing, which is denied by other witnesses. I have Sgt. Hertz in close confinement awaiting instruction from the Maj. Gen'l Comdg" [Commanding]. John R. Coxe, 5th U.S. Volunteers.

92. NARA M1017. Roll 45. Record Group 94. Pvt. Solomon Hurtz, Company "E," 5 Reg't U.S. Vols., Muster-out Roll, Ft. Kearny, N. T. [Nebraska Territory].

93. NARA 1017. Roll 42. Record Group 94. "Inventory of the effects of Private John R. Coxe, January 19, 1866."

94. NARA M1017. Roll 49. Record Group 94. "Volunteer Enlistment" document, Alton, Illinois, Military Prison. James R. Pittard, 5th U.S. Volunteers.

95. NARA M1017. Roll 49. Record Group 94. Contains Pittard's Union service record.

96. Dee Brown, *Galvanized Yankees*, p. 210.

97. The approximate number of Galvanized Yankees is arrived at by using the following figures from individual military service records: First U.S. Volunteers, 1867; Second U.S. Volunteers, 1366; Third U.S. Volunteers 852; Fourth U.S. Volunteers, 801; Fifth U.S. Volunteers, 1685; and Sixth U.S. Volunteers, 1526, for a total of the six regiments of 8,097 men. There is some duplication of service records because of different spellings. The names and service records also include regular U.S. Army officers and enlisted men. I estimate these duplicate records and total of officers and enlisted men from the Regular Army at about 10 per cent of the 8,097 total, leaving 7,289 in the six regiments. If we add about 1,000 other Galvanized Yankees in various other regiments of the Union forces, we reach a total of 8,289. This is a conservative figure. Other writers have made other estimates ranging from 6,000 to as high as 12,000, but these estimates do not give details about how they were figured.

98. "A Parting Word," Oct. 12, 1865.

99. NARA M1017. Roll 1. Record Group 94. 1st U.S. Volunteers, Enoch G. Adams.

Appendix

The Robert Denney Spreadsheet

Before he died on June 22, 2002, Major Robert E. Denney (Retired) created a potentially very useful spreadsheet about "Galvanized Yankees." The spreadsheet, containing many thousands of lines of data from National Archives records, was fashioned over years of research by Major Denney. This decorated Marine and Army veteran was fascinated by the history of the ex-Confederate soldiers captured in the Civil War and placed in Northern military prisons where they took the oath of loyalty to the Union Army. These former Confederates went West to serve in the First through the Sixth U.S. Volunteer Infantry Regiments and also served in the U.S. Navy. The volunteer Army regiments were mainly made up of ex-Confederate soldiers under command of Union officers and Union non-commissioned officers. Other Galvanized Yankees saw combat aboard Navy ships.

The Major had an outstanding combat record himself. He was a Marine in China in the mid-1940's and served in other military activities, making secret missions behind the North Korean lines in the Korean War. He was also a helicopter pilot in Vietnam.

He was nearly killed when a bullet passed through his helmet but missed his skull. The veteran entered military service out of high school as a Marine. Denney later on joined the Army and eventually was promoted to the rank of major, in helicopter navigation systems. His decorations included the Silver Star, Bronze Star with "V" Device, Distinguished Flying Cross and two Purple Hearts.

Major Denney retired from military service, and as a civilian he worked his way through Strayer College, which specialized in adult education. There he received his bachelor's and master's degrees in computer science.

He showed a love for research on the Civil War and wrote several books about the war. He was eulogized for his military service when he was buried with full military honors at Arlington National Cemetery.

He labored on records of Galvanized Yankees for several years at the National Archives in Washington, D. C., tracing Confederates in Union prisons and their records as Galvanized Yankees in the Union Army in the West and in the U.S. Navy. These records were scattered and often difficult to find.

Major Denney's spreadsheet consolidated all he could find about thousands of Galvanized Yankees and their Confederate and Union service. Major Denney completed the spreadsheet before he died from lung cancer. In 2014 I found a mention in an online blog about Major Denney's work and learned that his friend, Dr. Tom Lowry, M. D., had the spreadsheet on disks. Lowry sent copies of the disks to me.

Denney's spreadsheet, however, was prepared in an early version of Microsoft Access, a now-obsolete version of the computer program. I hired two computer specialists to open the spreadsheet. Their success was only partial. We retrieved some information about hundreds of ex-Confederate Galvanized Yankees, but couldn't read the entire spreadsheet. We didn't find any conversion program because the original program was so old, being in use in the 1990s.

I took the text we deciphered and using the "find" command in several spreadsheet programs, including Excel, was able to obtain records of 52 Galvanized Yankees born in Clarke County, Georgia, and its adjacent counties. Their information was buried in more than 51,000 rows of data, with many variables. This fragmentary information has unlocked some key details for this book. I checked Major Denney's entries about Clarke County area Galvanized Yankees against military records in the National Archives or elsewhere.

66 *Appendix*

His work was quite accurate. His data led to many official records, both Confederate and Union, and it made it possible for me to give readers a picture of what being a Galvanized Yankee was like.

This book doesn't give a complete image of Galvanized Yankees from this area of Georgia. There is, however, enough information to present an accurate sketch of their times as Confederate soldiers shifting their allegiance, at least for the time of their service, to their Union ex-enemies.

If researchers have an interest in Denney's Galvanized Yankee data, they may contact me at alhester@earthlink.net about how to obtain disk copies for more efforts at decoding them with modern programs or conversions. They contain a wealth of information.

Al Hester, Athens, Georgia, March 29, 2015

Acknowledgments

I am grateful to recognize persons giving their time and effort which helped make this book a reality.

First, I should acknowledge the achievement of the late Major Robert Denney (Retired) who worked hard gathering information at the National Archives concerning Galvanized Yankees. I was unable to decode all of his spreadsheet completed about 25 years ago about the Galvanized Yankees. The parts I could decode made it possible for me to find the records of Athens area Confederate soldiers in Northern prisons who sought their freedom by swearing allegiance to the Union Army.

Secondly, I'd like to thank Dr. Tom Lowry, M.D., who made the Denney spreadsheet available. He also gave me much help when I was researching the Galvanized Yankees from the Athens area.

Glenda Patton aided greatly by making family history available concerning John M. Whitmire, born in Jackson County, Georgia. Without her aid, there would be no photographs or family details about this man who became a Galvanized Yankee and drew a Union military pension. Lynn Spratling also generously made Whitmire information available.

Richard Mayo was of much help, furnishing a photo of Galvanized Yankee Henry H. Lancaster, born in Jackson County. Sarah Locklin Taylor was very helpful providing family history on another Galvanized Yankee, Absalom Jones of Morgan County.

Also giving valuable help in obtaining old photographs of Galvanized Yankees in the Athens area were David Morin, Penny K. Stowe, Darrel A. Ronshausen and Ron Jones.

Anthony Barkdoll and Kenneth Taylor gave professional computer aid to decipher some of the Denney spreadsheet.

Expressing general interest or making suggestions for book content were Janet Patterson, Ashley Simpson, Amy Andrews, Mary Ann Abbe, James K. Reap, and Carol Lee Hilewick. Charlotte Marshall also gave support and encouragement for writing the book, although she was concurrently very busy with her own book interests.

Anne Richmond Boston, an excellent graphics and layout artist, has contributed greatly to the attractiveness of the book.

Conoly Hester, my wife, and Pat McAlexander, Larry Dendy and Theresa M. Flynn edited the book, making it more readable. We won't add these extra names to the index at this late date.

If I have left out anyone, please accept my apologies!

Al Hester

About the Author

Al Hester has lived in Athens for forty-three years, and is constantly amazed by the rich history and culture of the town and Clarke County. He has written or edited several books and articles about the history of Athens and surrounding areas.

In 2011 his book, *Enduring Legacy: Clarke County, Georgia's Ex-Slave Legislators, Madison Davis and Alfred Richardson*, won the Athens-Clarke Heritage Foundation's Outstanding Publication or Program Award. He also edited *Athens Memories: The WPA Federal Writers' Project Interviews*, which contains interviews with Athens citizens and their recollections dating back to slavery and through to the 1930's. He is the co-author with Conoly Hester, his wife, of *Athens: Celebrating 200 Years at the Millennium*, sponsored by the Athens-Clarke Heritage Foundation, Inc.

Dr. Hester retired in 1997 as director of the James M. Cox, Jr., Center for International Mass Communication Training and Research, which he founded, at the University of Georgia. For eight years he was instrumental in obtaining grants from the James M. Cox, Jr., Foundation to establish and operate the Center. The Center trained several thousand journalists and students, mainly in 36 foreign countries, especially in developing nations or former Communist countries.

Receiving his Ph.D. in mass communication from the University of Wisconsin, Madison, graduating with highest honors, he came to teach in 1972 at the Henry W. Grady College of Journalism and Mass Communication. He was department head of the News-Editorial

Department for eight years and also taught reporting, editing, magazine writing and international communications. He is director emeritus of the Cox Center and professor emeritus of the Grady College of Journalism and Mass Communication.

A native Texan, Dr. Hester was education reporter, local government reporter, assistant city editor and city editor of the *Dallas Times Herald* in Dallas, Texas. He received his bachelor's degree in journalism at Southern Methodist University, and his master's degree in mass communication at the University of Wisconsin, Madison.

The author or editor of about a dozen books, Dr. Hester is also an active magazine free-lancer. He has researched and written several studies on Latin American colonial newspapers and also a study of violence in front page content of leading U.S. newspapers over 50 years' time. Dr. Hester is the author of several articles for *The Athens Historian*, publication of the Athens Historical Society.

After retiring, he founded the Green Berry Press, which has published several history books involving Athens and other parts of Georgia. Dr. Hester has written many academic and popular free-lance articles. He serves as head of the History and Research Committee for Gospel Pilgrim Cemetery, a restored African-American Cemetery in East Athens, and has written a historical booklet about that cemetery. Dr. Hester is a member of the Athens-Clarke Heritage Foundation and served on its education committee. He also belongs to the Athens Historical Society and the Clarke-Oconee Genealogical Society. He is a member of St. Gregory's Episcopal Church, Athens, and has served two terms on its vestry.

He and Conoly have two children, Katherine L. Hester of Atlanta, and Albert C. Hester of Columbia, South Carolina. They also have two grandchildren, Ava and Paloma Carubia.

Index

CPSIA information can be obtained at www.ICGtesting.com
Printed in the USA
LVIW01n1058241115
463911LV00005B/5

* 9 7 8 0 9 9 6 6 3 9 9 0 3 *